Discover This

Discover This

Tzvi Gluckin

ISBN: 978-0-9845856-4-9

First Edition, September 2010
Second Edition (Revised and Updated), December 2011

You can reach the author at tzvi.gluckin@gmail.com

Typesetting, layout, and design by Larissa Zaretsky

Cover by Tzvi Lebetkin

Appendix:
Torah Codes: Responding to the Critics by Rabbi Moshe Zeldman and *The Accuracy of Our Written Torah* by Rabbi Dovid Lichtman are reprinted here with permission from the authors.

Printed in Israel
15 14 13 12 11   10 9 8 7 6 5 4 3 2

For I know that the hypnotized never lie. Do you?

- The Who, "Won't Get Fooled Again"

April 28, 2010 | 14 Nissan, 5770

We are thrilled that Tzvi Gluckin has written a book based on his presentation of the Discovery Seminar. Discovery is one of the oldest and most important programs Aish HaTorah offers. It addresses many of the difficult questions people have about the authorship of the Torah and it offers compelling answers that do not necessitate a leap of blind faith. Tzvi has an uncanny ability to express difficult concepts in a deceptively simple style – a style that is particularly appealing to college students and other young people – and this version of Discovery is no exception. Tzvi has produced an authoritative text. It is well documented, accurate, easy to read, and easy to understand. As one of our students put it, "This book is like having Tzvi standing in your room, giving you a personal Discovery presentation."

We know you will enjoy this book as much as we did and we wish Tzvi the best of luck in all his efforts on behalf of *Klal Yisroel*.

Sincerely,

Eric Coopersmith
CEO of Aish International and on behalf of the
Aish Discovery Program

Table of Contents

Introduction ℵ 1

Know It! ℵ 5

Outside Verification ℵ 11
How Did That Happen? The Contradictory Nature of Jewish Survival

You Do the Math ℵ 35
The Story of the Torah Codes

Identifying Information ℵ 69
The Pig's Foot: Information Only the Author Knows

Transmission ℵ 73
A Funny Thing Happened on the Way From Mount Sinai:
The Jewish Experience at Mount Sinai

Transmission ℵ 93
The Accuracy of the Torah's Transmission

Control ℵ 101
Esther, Purim, and the Nazis

What do you think? ℵ 113

Appendix ℵ 117

   Torah Codes: Responding to the Critics ℵ 117
   by Rabbi Moshe Zeldman

   The Accuracy of Our Written Torah ℵ 127
   by Rabbi Dovid Lichtman

Endnotes ℵ 135

Acknowledgements ℵ 145

Acknowledgements to the Second Edition ℵ 147

About the Author ℵ 149

Introduction

It was 1993. I was twenty-five. I had an apartment in Brooklyn. I was comfortable, but I wanted to experience new things. I decided to travel. I hit the road in May and escaped New York. I saw trendy Western Europe and the newly liberated East. I went to Turkey. I saw Greece. And six months later I was in Israel. It was my first time. I started in Haifa, but by the end of my first day I was in Jerusalem.

Jerusalem was cool. It was old, hot, mystical, and exciting. I decided to stay in Jerusalem until I was ready to see something else. After that I would check out the rest of Israel. And then I would move on. I didn't know what to see next, but it didn't matter. Maybe I would visit the Far East. Or maybe I would go home. But I didn't really want to go home.

I stayed at a youth hostel in Jerusalem's Old City. It was an interesting place. It was free for Jewish travelers. The staff was Jewish. The guests were Jewish. Everyone was sarcastic, complained, and liked to argue. It was great. And the Old City was more than just a tourist attraction. It was a vibrant spiritual center. It had the Western Wall, ancient synagogues, and many yeshivas. (A yeshiva is like a university for Judaism. It is a place to study the Torah, Talmud, Jewish philosophy, Hebrew, and other Jewish topics.) Some of the yeshivas offered introductory classes. The classes were free. You usually got a free meal and the coffee was free, too. And the classes were interesting.

The staff at my hostel encouraged me to go to the classes. I did. Why not? I heard cool ideas, drank free coffee, and ate free food. After the classes I hung out at the hostel and had deep – and usually pretentious – conversations with the other guests. It was fun.

But there was one class everyone talked about. It was a three-day seminar. It was taught in an old building just across from the Western Wall and it wasn't free. It cost $90.

It was called, "Discovery."

Everyone – the staff at the hostel, the other guests, the teachers at the yeshivas – talked about Discovery. They were wild about it. "What is it about?" I asked. "It is amazing. Do it. You will love it." They said.

Ok. I asked around. Word on the street was that Discovery proved that God wrote the Torah. That made me nervous. I wasn't sure if I believed in God and it never occurred to me that God wrote a book. It sounded like hocus-pocus. And I wasn't interested in an intense lecture about religion. I liked the laid-back classes at the yeshivas. But I thought about it. I had nothing to lose. I was brave. So I took the seminar despite my reservations.

And I am glad I did.

Discovery didn't prove that God wrote the Torah. It wasn't about that. Discovery was about Judaism. It was about thinking. It was about Jewish history. And it was about me.

Discovery was about a heritage I took for granted, didn't know much about, and based on assumptions that weren't correct. It gave me a new vocabulary. It gave me a different way to think about faith and religion. It gave me a new appreciation for who I was and where I came from.

And it gave me a reason to ask questions. I left the Discovery Seminar with more questions than I had when I started. That was a good thing. It forced me to think. It made me uncomfortable. And it challenged my assumptions.

Not bad for three days and $90.

This book is what I learned. It is the ideas I first heard in 1993. It isn't a live seminar. It is a book. And it isn't three days of classes, but that is good. A book is slower. You have time to process your thoughts, discuss it with your friends, look it up online, and formulate your questions.

The first section – Know It – is definitions. Can an intelligent, thinking person believe that God wrote the Torah? It defines faith, knowledge, and the criteria for belief.

The rest of the book is evidence. Specifically, it presents five classes of evidence:

- ✕ Outside Verification: Evidence – independent of Judaism – that suggests that God wrote the Torah.
- ✕ Codes: Information hidden in the text of the Torah. How did it get there?
- ✕ Identifying Information: Evidence similar to your banking PIN or password, only you know it.
- ✕ Transmission: The text of the Torah hasn't changed in 3,000 years. How do you know?
- ✕ Control: The author controls history. He can manipulate events to work out the way he wants them to.

Discover This. It will challenge your assumptions. It may make you uncomfortable. It should get you to ask questions. And asking questions is good. You won't agree with everything. And you won't disagree with everything.

And that's good, too.

Discover This will make you think. Think about what you believe and why you believe it. And think about what it means to be Jewish.

Know It!

The Torah is the most important Jewish book. Everything Jewish is in it: Jewish values, ethics, morals, history, holidays, traditions, and laws. It is the backbone of Judaism. And it has been with the Jews since the beginning.

It is also influential. Other religions are based on it. Many rights, freedoms, philosophies, and liberties are derived from it. It was the first book ever printed. And it was translated into hundreds of languages.

Who wrote it?

The Torah claims it was written by God. The book says so. But think about it. Can a normal, intelligent, rational, levelheaded, thinking person believe that God wrote a book? That is a crazy sounding question. The Torah is not a crazy book; it exerts a lot of influence. It is not the outdated epic of an ancient people. It is alive and well. A lot of people believe it. And it claims to be the word of God.

Is it?

Many people take a leap of faith. But blind faith is uncomfortable. It isn't rational. A thinking person needs evidence. How much evidence do you need?

Think about how much evidence you need to believe anything. Maybe you don't need a lot of evidence to believe that God wrote the Torah. Or maybe you do. Different beliefs are based on different sets of criteria. The amount of evidence depends on the idea, how important it is, and where it comes from.

5

Most of your beliefs fall into one of four categories:

- ℵ The ideas you accept because your society believes them
- ℵ The ideas you accept on faith
- ℵ The ideas you accept based on evidence
- ℵ And the things you know

Not every belief is the same. Some beliefs require more evidence than others. And the amount of evidence is what distinguishes between categories.

Which category applies to the Torah? Study the description of each category and decide.

Socialization

The first category is what your society believes. It includes the ideas you grew up with. You take these ideas for granted. You consider them common sense. You accept them at face value. You don't question the assumptions they are based on. And they are pervasive.

These ideas are a part of your life. They affect the way you speak, how you act on a date, how you dress for a job interview, the sports you like, and your taste in food. They are everywhere. They also affect more fundamental attitudes like your relationship to religion, what you consider basic rights and freedoms, your work ethic, your politics, and the way you think other people should be treated. You probably don't question these beliefs.

But think about it.

Other people have different beliefs. They think differently. They act differently. They probably take their beliefs for granted, too. Who's right?

That's hard to say.

Most people accept a set of ideas they assume to be true. They learned these ideas from their society. Different societies, cultures, communities, and groups believe different things. Is your society right? Maybe a different society is right.

How do you know?

Faith

The second category is faith. Faith is belief without proof. It is emotional. It is blind. And it isn't rational.

Faith is the reason people get ripped off. It is the reason they trust con artists. It is the reason they buy lottery tickets. It is the reason they get stuck in horrible relationships. Faith is when you trust your desires, not your brains. But it isn't always bad. It helps people get through tough times and it gives them something to believe in.

And faith is natural. Sometimes you are confronted with a situation, see the evidence, and still don't believe it.

Did you ever go to a funeral? Notice that the mourners don't cry uncontrollably. They cry at significant points during the service: when the body is brought out, during the eulogies, when they say the prayer for the dead, and when dirt is shoveled onto the grave.

The reason the mourner cries at these significant points – and not uncontrollably – is because he *believes* his loved one is still alive. He knows he isn't, but he doesn't believe it. It isn't real. He doesn't *feel* it.

And that's faith. The mourner feels what he wants to believe, in spite of the evidence. He cries at points that break his faith – evidence that proves his loved one really died – and it hurts.

Belief

The next category is belief. Belief is a conviction based on evidence: the stronger the evidence, the stronger the conviction.

Most legal systems are based on belief. The judge didn't see the crime. He was presented evidence. Based on the evidence he decided if the defendant was guilty. He sent the defendant to jail – or even recommended the death penalty – based on the evidence. And even if the evidence was overwhelming, the judge didn't know like the witnesses did. They saw the event. He didn't.

Is the earth round?

Look at the evidence. Do you get jetlag when you fly from one part of the world to another? Have you called a friend in a different time zone? Have you seen a ship dip below the horizon? Have you seen the earth's shadow during a lunar eclipse?[1] Based on the evidence, most people conclude that the earth is round.

Is your mother really your mother?

Look at the evidence. Do you look like her? Have you asked your father? What do your grandparents say? If you believe she is your mother, it is probably based on the evidence as well.

Could you be wrong? Of course. The evidence isn't foolproof. But unless you get your mother to admit she's a liar, or you go into space and see the flat earth, the evidence is strong enough to support your convictions.

Belief isn't 100%. But in most cases – and based on the evidence – belief can lead to strong convictions.

Knowledge

The fourth category is knowledge. Knowledge is an intuitive perception. It is based on an overabundance of evidence. You know something because the evidence is overwhelming.

Have you been to China?

If you answered "no," does China exist? How do you know? (If you answered "yes," pretend.)

Consider the evidence. China is on the map. It is in the news. You know people who visited. You have eaten Chinese food. You own products that were made there. You know Chinese people.

Think about it. Maybe you were duped. It is a global conspiracy. Every mapmaker, reporter, manufacturer, "Chinese person," and tourist is in on it. "China" is a giant fiction. It doesn't exist.

Does that sound reasonable?

I don't think so. China exists. You know it does. The evidence is overwhelming. It is preposterous to suggest that it doesn't. And you know China exists – you know it for a fact – and you never need to visit to prove it. The amount of evidence is massive. It is silly to suggest that the entire world is lying.

What about the Torah? Did God write it? What is the basis for belief? Is it based on socialization, faith, belief, or knowledge?

Most people say faith. But calling Judaism a faith-based religion is the result of social conditioning. In the West, Christianity is the dominant religion. Christianity dominates Western thought, culture, philosophy, and literature. When a Western person thinks "religion," he means "Christianity." And Christianity is faith-based.

Judaism isn't Christianity. Judaism is a different religion. And Judaism demands evidence.

Think about it.

Jews are called the people of the book. Jews value education. Jews like thinking, arguing, debating, and being right. Knowledge is a big part of Jewish culture. "Know before whom you stand," is a phrase found in many synagogues. It is usually carved in stone and written in big letters. It doesn't say believe, hope, or have faith in. It says, "Know." That is a big deal.

The Torah demands knowledge as well. Look at this quote from the Book of Deuteronomy:

> Know this day and place it on your heart that God is the only God – in the heavens above and on the earth below – there is none other.[2]

Faith and society are not good enough. If you want to believe that God wrote the Torah, you need evidence. And knowledge is king.

What about belief?

Rabbi Moshe Chaim Luzzatto was a great rabbi, philosopher, and Jewish thinker. He lived in the eighteenth century. He was born in Italy, but spent most of his adult life in Amsterdam. He died in Israel at the age of forty. He was a prolific writer and his books are influential. One of his most important books was *The Way of God*. In *The Way of God*, Rabbi Luzzatto discussed Judaism as a system. He talked about God, the Torah, the Commandments, prophecy, and many other ideas. Look at what he said was the first thing every Jew must do:

> Every Jew must believe *and* know.[3]

Both: you need belief and knowledge. Knowledge is the goal. Belief is the first step. And belief is based on evidence. Don't take a leap of faith. Gather evidence. Study the evidence. Decide if it makes sense. If it does, believe based on the evidence.

That is how you make most decisions.

How do you buy a house? Do you pick a town at random and choose the first house you find? No. You gather evidence and decide if it makes sense. You do research. You research the town. You research the job market. You check out the neighborhood. You research the taxes. And you check out the schools.

When you find a house, you take a good look at it. You look at the rooms. You check out the basement, kitchen, attic, and yard. You find out about the sewer, septic, electricity, heating system, and water. You ask about asbestos. You hire an inspector. You have the value of the house appraised. You gather as much evidence as you can before you buy a house.

You gather evidence for every big decision. What would you do if your car made a funny noise, you took it to a mechanic, and the mechanic waved his hands over the hood and dug your car's vibes? What if he told you that the vibes felt like a faulty transmission? Would you trust him?

Of course not.

A good mechanic gives evidence. He puts the car on a lift, opens the hood, and runs a few tests. You wouldn't trust him – and you wouldn't pay him – if he didn't.

You gather evidence for small decisions, too.

Most people won't go to a movie or restaurant without a recommendation. They won't buy a toaster, camera, TV, suitcase, or lawnmower without a recommendation either. Most people need evidence.

You gather evidence. You decide to do things or buy things based on the evidence. You won't do it without it. That is how you are made.

Did God create man? Pretend you agree. Man needs evidence. He demands evidence. His decisions are based on evidence. And that is the way God made him. God made man to think, decide, choose, and make smart decisions based on evidence.

Think about it. God created a thinker. If that is true, does it make sense that man demands evidence in every situation, except when it comes to religion? That's silly. If man needs evidence, he needs evidence for religion and belief in God. He needs evidence to believe that God wrote the Torah, too. Look at the evidence and decide for yourself. Subject the Torah to the same standards you use when making any decision. That makes sense.

The rest of this book presents evidence. Like I said in the introduction, it presents five classes of evidence: Outside Verification, Codes, Indentifying Information, Transmission, and Control.

Each class is a piece in a puzzle. Look at each class of evidence. Think about it. Does it make sense? Compare it to the other pieces. Do they add up? Is the evidence compelling?

Read the book. Think about the evidence. And decide for yourself. Did God write the Torah? It is a crazy sounding question. But the answer isn't crazy. Maybe you have to take a leap of faith.

But maybe you don't.

Maybe you can believe it based on the evidence.

Outside Verification

How Did That Happen?
The Contradictory Nature of
Jewish Survival

Are you Jewish? If so, Jewish survival doesn't surprise you. You exist. You survived. Enough said.

But you should be impressed.

Jewish survival doesn't make sense. Look at Jewish history: exile, persecution, oppression, forced conversions, assimilation, and intermarriage. Nations don't survive these things.

The Jews should be gone.

Where are the Babylonians, Romans, and ancient Egyptians? They ruled the world. They built great empires. They were wealthy. They had massive armies. And then they were conquered and disappeared.

History is full of examples. A powerful nation conquers another. The conquering power dominates the losers. They tax them, seize their property, outlaw their religion, arrest their leaders, exile their elite, and subject them to new laws and ideas. The conquered people lose their identity. They forget their language. They adopt a new religion. And they assimilate. Within a few generations they vanish. Their food, culture, habits, and tastes disappear.

They even stop using their names. When was the last time you met a Julius?

But not the Jews.

Jews are different. The Jews survived in spite of conquest, exile, assimilation, intermarriage, and even ignorance of their heritage.

How did that happen?

Take it a step further. The Jews didn't just survive. They made a big noise.

The Jews are not a meek, quiet, inconsequential people. They are noted in every field, business, discipline, craft, innovation, and area you can think of. They changed the way the world thinks about religion. Jews are everywhere, into everything, and usually at the forefront of whatever is going on.

I am not the first person to notice this. Look at what Mark Twain said:

> The Egyptian, the Babylonian, and the Persian rose, filled the planet with sound and splendor, then faded to dream-stuff and passed away. The Greek and Roman followed, made a vast noise and they are gone. Other peoples have sprung up, and held their torch high for a time, but it burned out and they sit in twilight now or have vanished. The Jew saw them all, beat them all, and is now what he always was, exhibiting no decadence, no infirmities of age, no weakening of his parts, no slowing of his energies, no dulling of his alert and aggressive mind. All things are mortal, but the Jew. All other forces pass, but he remains. What is the secret of his immortality?[4]

Impressive.

Leo Tolstoy goes even further:

> The Jew is the emblem of eternity. He who neither slaughter nor torture thousands of years could destroy, he who neither fire, nor sword, nor inquisition was able to wipe off the face of the earth. He who was the first to produce the Oracles of God. He who has been for so long the Guardian of Prophecy and has transmitted it to the rest of the world. Such a nation cannot be destroyed. The Jew is as everlasting as Eternity itself.[5]

And look at this quote from John Adams (second President of the United States):

I will insist the Hebrews have [contributed] more to civilize men than any other nation. If I was an atheist and believed in blind eternal fate, I should still believe that fate had ordained the Jews to be the most essential instrument for civilizing the nations ... They are the most glorious nation that ever inhabited this Earth. The Romans and their empire were but a bubble in comparison to the Jews. They have given religion to three-quarters of the globe and have influenced the affairs of mankind more and more happily than any other nation, ancient or modern.[6]

The Jews survived. They changed the world. Their influence is everywhere. They did it with their hands tied behind their back.

Jews are great. Everyone says so.

The Torah says the Jews are great too.

Are you surprised? The Torah is a pro-Jewish book. You expect it to love Jews.

But the Torah also says that the Jews will be persecuted, exiled, dispersed, hated, and a few other terrible things.

Did you expect the Torah to say that too?

The Torah makes many statements about Jewish destiny. It predicts the Jews will be great but oppressed, influential but despised, and an eternal people but hated. These are contradictions. Most groups are one or the other, not both. The Torah claims both.

And the Torah is specific. It isn't vague. It makes explicit – yet contradictory – predictions about Jewish history. It says the Jewish people will be eternal yet dispersed across the globe, few in number, and hated. In spite of these things, they will be a light unto the nations. After years of exile they will return to Israel. And when they return the land will blossom, even though it was unproductive when they didn't live there.

If you wrote the Torah, would you make these predictions?

The Torah is a religious book. It claims to be the word of God. That makes these predictions prophecies.

I know what you are thinking. Prophecies are weird, esoteric, Nostradamus-type things. They are poetic and allegorical; thick in metaphor, hyperbole, and open for interpretation. You twist them to predict whatever you want.

And the Torah has prophecies like this. Most religious books do. You will find mystical, esoteric, wild prophecies in the Book of

Revelation, the Maya Codices, the Book of Mormon, the Koran, the Egyptian Book of the Dead, the Bhagavad-Gita, and anywhere else you look. Religious books are filled with this stuff.

But the contradictory claims the Torah makes about Jewish history are not like this. They are explicit. They are in clear, unambiguous language. And they were made at the start of Jewish history. Before the Jews did anything.

How long ago was that?

According to Jewish tradition, the Torah is about 3,300 years old. The Jewish people gathered at Mount Sinai in 1313 BCE.[7] God spoke to them and gave them the Torah. That was a long time ago.

If you don't trust Jewish tradition, you still have to say the Torah is old. About 2,300 years ago, the Greeks conquered Israel. They translated the Torah into Greek. The translation is called the Septuagint.[8] In the Septuagint's introduction, the Torah is called "the ancient book of the Jews." The Greeks thought the Torah was old too.

The Septuagint is significant. The Torah joined the ranks of world literature. You didn't have to learn Hebrew to read it. And it is unlikely the Torah was changed, edited, or modified once it was translated. Too many people had access to it.

But if you don't like the Septuagint, the Torah is at least as old as Christianity. Christianity is built on Judaism. The Christian bible is the *New* Testament to Judaism's *Old*. That makes the Torah at least 2,000 years old. It is hard to say the Torah was changed after the Christians accepted it.

I think it is fair to say that the Torah's contradictory predictions are at least 2,000 years old.

Mark Twain, Leo Tolstoy, and John Adams marveled at Jewish survival. They would be stunned to learn that Jewish survival was predicted before it happened, at least 2,000 years ago.

How about you?

1. Eternal Nation

The Jews are eternal. Not an unusual claim. Many groups have been around for a long time. The Chinese, Indians, and Arabs are ancient peoples too.

But look at the common features of nationhood. Most nations share a common land, language, and history. Do the Jews?

Common land. What is the land of the Jews? Most people say Israel. Is that true?

Take a look.

Most Jews were not born in Israel. Most Jews are not from Israel. And many Jews have never been to Israel.

America has one of the world's largest Jewish populations. Most Jewish Americans have never been to Israel. And most are not planning a trip to Israel.

How is Israel the common land of the Jews?

Modern Israel is a recent phenomenon. Only about 25,000 Jews lived there in 1900. For most of Jewish history, most Jews lived everywhere except Israel, including Europe, North Africa, South America, North America, and the Middle East.[9] Israel was last the common land – the place where most Jewish people were born, lived, worked, and died – in biblical times.

I grew up in North Jersey. My parents are from the New York area, too. So are my grandparents. My aunts, uncles, and cousins lived in New York, New Jersey, and Connecticut. It never occurred to me that Jews lived anywhere else.

I decided to travel when I was twenty-five years old. It was the first time I left America. I was gone for seven and a half years. My first stop was Europe. The first city I visited was Amsterdam. I stayed in Amsterdam for a few weeks and played guitar on the streets to earn money. I made about $40 an hour.

I was friendly with the other street musicians. One of them was from India. He played the violin. One day he said to me, "You are Jewish."

"Yes I am," I said, "How did you know?"

"I am Jewish too," He said.

That rocked my world.

His family was originally from Portugal. They fled in the 16th century at the time of the Portuguese Inquisition. They spent time in Turkey, the Middle East, and finally India.

I traveled and met other non-New York Jews. I met Jews from Iran, Canada, Uzbekistan, Kansas, Chile, South Africa, New Zealand, Sweden, Ethiopia, and Iowa. Jews are from everywhere.

It is hard to name a place where Jews haven't lived in the last 2,000 years. The only land common to all Jews is Earth.

Common language. What is the Jewish language? Most people say Hebrew. Is that true? Many Jews don't speak Hebrew. Some can read it. Many can pronounce the letters. Some can't even do that.

Eastern European Jews speak Yiddish. Yiddish is a crazy hybrid language combining German, Polish, Russian, Hebrew, and Aramaic expressions from the Talmud. Some Jews still speak Yiddish. Most don't.

I try to use Yiddish words. My Yiddish-speaking friends think it is funny. I can't follow a conversation in Yiddish. I can't read it either. Can you?

Jews from Spain and North Africa speak Ladino. Ladino is a combination of Spanish, Arabic, Hebrew, and Aramaic expressions from the Talmud. I don't know how many people still speak Ladino.

Do the Jewish people have a common language?

The last time most Jews spoke Hebrew was biblical times – back when the Jews last lived in Israel. Hebrew hasn't been a common language for Jews since then. Nowadays the language most Jews speak is English.

And that will probably change, too.

Common history. Do Jews share a common history?

Other nations do. The French share a common history.

French people live in France, speak French, eat French food, were conquered by the Nazis, invaded in World War One, conquered Europe under Napoleon, survived the blood bath of the French Revolution, and lived under a French monarch going back to Charlemagne. This history is common to all French people.

The people of most nations share a common history. They share a set of experiences that affected most of their group. The experiences were unique to them. It is their history.

Except the Jews.

Jews from Europe were blamed for the Black Plague, killed during the Crusades, forced to live in ghettos, targeted in pogroms, and murdered in the Holocaust. They also lived through emancipation, the rise of Humanism, and Enlightenment.

The Jews from North Africa and the Middle East didn't have these experiences. They were forced to convert to Islam, labeled *Dhimi* (second-class citizens), forced to wear badges that identified them as Jewish, and evicted from their homes after the Israeli War of Independence in 1948.[10] The dominant religion in the places they lived – Islam – didn't go through a reformation. They weren't exposed to Humanism, Enlightenment, and the rise of science. And their host governments were not progressive or liberal.

The history of European and Middle Eastern Jews is so different, that in 1961/2 – during the Eichmann Trial – Jews from the Middle East were used as guards, but not Jews from Europe. The Israelis felt that a Middle Eastern Jew was less likely to murder Eichmann before his trial ended.[11]

The Jews lived as a minority group in many different countries. Their lives were wrapped up in the history of their host nation. The history of each Jewish community is unique and most Jews do not share a common history.

But they are still Jews.

Jewish people are distinct. A Jew is a Jew. A Jew from Poland is as Jewish as a Jew from Yemen. And they are distinct without a common land, language, or history. The Jews are considered a separate people. The Jews are a minority in every country they live in. They don't blend in or disappear.

If you really think about it, the Jews are eternal. The Jews remained a distinct people for at least 2,000 years. And they did it without the common features of nationhood.

You should be impressed. Mark Twain, Leo Tolstoy, and John Adams were.

And at least 2,000 years ago, the Torah claimed the Jews would be eternal. God promised.

> And I will establish My covenant between Me and you and your descendants after you throughout their generations – an eternal covenant – to be your God and the God of your descendants after you.[12]

2. Exile

Nations don't travel. Germany never went on a road trip. Cambodia didn't go camping. Nations are associated with the places they live.

Exile is when the nation leaves home. Nations don't survive exile. Over time they assimilate and lose their identity.

Except the Jews. Jews live everywhere. And Jews are on the move.

Most Jews were not born in the same country as their great-grandparents.[13] They emigrated to avoid persecution, oppression, second-class status, special taxes, war, and mob violence. Sometimes they were forced out. Sometimes they went voluntarily.

It is unusual for Jews to stay put. They wander. Every four generations – for whatever reason – Jewish people move to a new home.

And the Jews are dispersed, too. You cannot name a place Jews don't live or didn't once live.

Can a nation survive exile and dispersion?

Look what happens.

The original exiles move to the new country and settle in an immigrant community (like Chinatown, Little Italy, and Brighton Beach in Brooklyn).

But their children want to fit in. They move to the suburbs, send their kids to public school, buy them TVs, send them to college, and raise them to be good citizens.

These children are indistinguishable from the natives.

American history is full of examples. Dwight D. Eisenhower was the 34th President of the United States. During World War II, he was the Supreme Commander of the Allied Invading Force. He led the invasion of Europe, conquered Germany, and defeated the Nazis.[14] He was responsible for the bombing of German cities.

But look at his last name: Eisenhower. His family was from Germany. Was he German or American? Did he cry when he bombed Dresden, Hamburg, or Mainz?

I doubt it. He was an American. It doesn't matter if his grandparents drank beer, ate bratwurst, and wore suspenders. His blood was red, white, and blue. He went to West Point. He led the U.S. Army. He was the 34th President. He was as American as apple pie.

The Eisenhower story is typical. Many Jewish families have a similar story. Jews are not immune to assimilation. Yet the Jews are still a distinct group. Exile and dispersion was not the end of the Jewish people.

The Torah claimed the Jews would be eternal. It also claimed they would be exiled.

> And you, I will scatter among the nations, at the point of My drawn sword, leaving your country desolate and your cities in ruins.[15]

If you wrote the Torah, would you claim both eternal nation and exile? The ideas contradict each other.

3. Few In Number

Would China survive exile? I think it would.

If for some reason the Chinese people were exiled from their land, they would survive. Why?

There are 1.3 billion Chinese people.

That is a lot of people. They would set up Chinese communities in every major city. In some places they would constitute a majority. They would continue to speak Chinese. Chinese people would continue to marry other Chinese people.

The Chinese don't need the country of China to survive. They would maintain a distinct identity and culture no matter where they live.

Do the Jews have this same advantage? Are there 1.3 billion Jews in the world? Is that the reason for Jewish survival in exile?

Depending on which study you trust, there are between 12 and 14 *million* Jews in the world.[16] That is not a lot of people. Nothing like 1.3 billion. It is a lot less than the populations of America, England, Zimbabwe, and Egypt too. It is less than most tribes, clans, religions, or ethnicities.

There are not many Jews in the world.

Take the higher number: 14 million. It is about 0.227% of the world's total population. Round that off to the nearest whole number.

Zero.

Statistically, the Jews don't exist.

The Jews and Chinese had similar populations a long time ago. What happened?

The Chinese population grew. Not surprising. People had children. Those children had children. The population wasn't ravaged by war or disease. And the population exploded. Look at other nations. Their populations didn't become huge like the Chinese, but they have many more people than they did 1,000 years ago. Population growth is natural. It's something you expect.

What about the Jews?

The Jewish population peaked at 18 million. For a nation as ancient as the Jewish people, that is a small number. And that peak was in 1939, before the Holocaust. After the Holocaust, the population was down to 12 million. Today it is between 12 and 14 million.

Why doesn't the Jewish population grow?

I once compared an American Jewish population study published in 1990 with one published in 2000. The number of Jews living in America in 2000 was almost exactly the same as the number in 1990.

How did that happen?

It is unusual that the American Jewish population didn't grow over a ten-year period. Even more unusual is that about 1 million[17] Jews from the former Soviet Union immigrated to America during those years.

How did the American Jewish population remain unchanged? And why hasn't the world Jewish population grown since the Holocaust?

Odd.

The Torah claims stagnant or negative population growth as another contradictory promise from God.

> And you shall remain few in number among the nations where God shall lead you.[18]

Eternal nation, but exiled and few in number: it doesn't add up.

4. Anti-Semitism

If you hate blacks, Asians, Arabs, Mexicans, or any other group, you are called a racist. If you hate Catholics, Muslims, rednecks, Hindus, or the poor, you are called a bigot.

If you hate Jews, you are called an anti-Semite.

Jew-hatred is unique. It has a special name. Wilhelm Marr – a German writer and notorious Jew-hater – coined the term in an anti-Semitic pamphlet he published in 1880.[19] Anti-Semitism is different from other types racism and bigotry. It is distinguished in four ways, specifically its intensity, longevity, irrationality, and universality.

Intensity. Jew-hatred is ferocious. Bigotry, bias, second-class status, quotas, and inconvenience often devolve into mob violence, mass killings, race laws, and government sanctioned persecution. Jewish villages, cities, towns, communities, and regions were destroyed during the Crusades, pogroms, the Black Plague, the Holocaust, and as the result of Blood Lible and other accusations. Jews were murdered, tortured, raped, lynched, and killed in the most horrible ways imaginable. Jew-hatred is more than segregation or oppression. It is intense. Jew-killers are passionate, bloodthirsty, vicious, and brutal.

Have other groups been persecuted? Have other groups been the victims of horrible atrocities?

Of course.

But no other nation, race, religion, group, or minority has been persecuted for as long, as consistently, and as intensely as the Jews. Anti-Semites don't hold back. Jewish history is one worst-case scenario after another.

Longevity. Anti-Semitism is not new. Jews have been hated for a long time. Jews were persecuted by all the great powers in history. The Persian, Greek, and Roman empires persecuted the Jews. The Catholic Church and the Islamic Caliphate persecuted the Jews. Jews were persecuted at the dawn of Christianity, throughout the Dark Ages, Middle Ages, Renaissance, Enlightenment, and into modern times.

You can't name a time in the last 2,000 years when Jews *weren't* persecuted.

Irrationality. Jews are hated for everything. Look at this quote:

> The uniqueness of anti-Semitism lies in the fact that no other people in the world have been charged simultaneously with alienation from society and with cosmopolitanism; with being capitalist exploiters and also revolutionary communists; with having a materialistic mentality or being a people of the book. We are accused of being both militant aggressors and cowardly pacifists; adherents to a superstitious religion and agents of modernism. We uphold a rigid law and are also morally decadent. We have a chosen people mentality and an inferior human nature; we are both arrogant and timid; individualist and communally adherent; we are guilty of both the crucifixion of Jesus to Christians and to others we are held to account for the invention of Christianity. *Everything and its opposite becomes an explanation for anti-Semitism.*[20]

Anti-Semitism is irrational. It doesn't make sense. It isn't logical. If you are Jewish, somebody hates you. You didn't do anything.

Anything and everything is a reason to hate Jews. Name another group accused of conspiracy to plan an entire century.[21]

Universal. Anti-Semitism is universal. Look at this list of places Jews were expelled from[22]:

250 Carthage
415 Alexandria
554 Diocese of Clement (France)
561 Diocese of Uzzes (France)
612 Visigoth Spain
642 Visigoth Empire
855 Italy
876 Sens
1012 Mainz
1182 France
1182 Germany
1276 Upper Bavaria
1290 England
1306 France
1322 France (again)
1348 Switzerland
1349 Heilbronn (Germany)
1349 Saxony
1349 Hungary
1360 Hungary
1370 Belgium
1380 Slovakia
1388 Strasbourg
1394 Germany
1394 France
1420 Lyons
1421 Austria
1424 Fribourg
1424 Zurich
1424 Cologne
1432 Savoy
1438 Mainz
1439 Augsburg
1442 Netherlands
1444 Netherlands
1446 Bavaria

1453 France
1453 Breslau
1454 Wurzburg
1462 Mainz
1483 Mainz
1484 Warsaw
1485 Vincenza (Italy)
1492 Spain
1492 Italy
1495 Lithuania
1496 Naples
1496 Portugal
1498 Nuremberg
1498 Navarre
1510 Brandenburg
1510 Prussia
1514 Strasbourg
1515 Genoa
1519 Regensburg
1533 Naples
1541 Naples
1542 Prague & Bohemia
1550 Genoa
1551 Bavaria
1555 Pesaro
1557 Prague
1559 Austria
1561 Prague
1567 Wurzburg
1569 Papal States
1571 Brandenburg
1582 Netherlands
1582 Hungary
1593 Brandenburg, Austria
1597 Cremona, Pavia & Lodi
1614 Frankfort
1615 Worms
1619 Kiev

1648 Ukraine
1648 Poland
1649 Hamburg
1654 Little Russia (Byelorussia)
1656 Lithuania
1669 Oran (North Africa)
1669 Vienna
1670 Vienna
1712 Sandomir
1727 Russia
1738 Wurtemburg
1740 Little Russia (Beylorus)
1744 Prague, Bohemia
1744 Slovakia
1744 Livonia
1745 Moravia
1753 Kovad (Lithuania)
1761 Bordeaux
1772 Deported to the Pale of Settlement (Poland/Russia)
1775 Warsaw
1789 Alsace
1804 Villages in Russia
1808 Villages & Countrysides (Russia)
1815 L'beck & Bremen
1815 Franconia, Swabia & Bavaria
1820 Bremen
1843 Russian Border Austria & Prussia
1862 Areas in the U.S. under General Grant's Jurisdiction
1866 Galatz, Romania
1880s Russia
1891 Moscow
1919 Bavaria (foreign born Jews)
1938-45 Nazi Controlled Areas
1948 Arab Countries

It is difficult to name a place that didn't ban Jews. And that is just a list of expulsions. Many nations that didn't kick the Jews out still taxed, enslaved, persecuted, oppressed, murdered, or humiliated their Jewish populations. No nation is immune.

Even the United States has a history of anti-Semitism. After the Civil War, General Grant banned Jews from Tennessee.[23] Quotas kept most Jews from the best universities[24] (this is the reason Brandeis University was established in 1948).[25] The best law firms barred Jews.[26] The list goes on.

Anti-Semitism is like no other form of bigotry. It is savage, irrational, and unusual. You wouldn't expect a group to survive this relentless, universal hatred.

But the Jews have.

And the Torah warned the Jews about it.

> And those of you who survive in the land of your enemies, I shall make so fainthearted that if leaves rustle behind them, they will flee headlong, as if from the sword, though no one pursues them. Stumbling over one another as if to escape a weapon, while no one is after them. So helpless will you be to take a stand against your foes. You shall perish among the nations and the land of your enemies shall consume you.[27]

5. Light Unto The Nations

Look at that quote from John Adams again:

> "[The Jews] have given religion to three-quarters of the globe and have influenced the affairs of mankind more and more happily than any other nation, ancient or modern."

Is he right?

Christianity and Islam are both based on Judaism. They are monotheistic faiths. They worship the Jewish God. They accept the Jewish prophets. They believe God spoke at Mount Sinai. They accept the values, ethics, morals, and principles of Judaism.

They don't accept everything – but if they did they would be Jewish. And they don't constitute three-quarters of the globe – John Adams's number is off – although each group has over a billion believers.

Impressive. More than two billion people believe something based on Judaism. How did that happen? The Jews are hated, oppressed, and persecuted. The Jews are few in number. The Jews are scattered to the ends of the earth. How did they influence so many people?

Pretend it is 2,000 years ago. You live in Rome. You own a villa near the Forum. You wear a toga. You own Jewish slaves. Your slaves feed you grapes.

Someone tells you that Rome will be different in the future. The Roman Empire will disappear. No one will worship the Roman gods. And Christianity will replace Roman religion.

Would you believe him?

No.

You would think he is crazy. Rome is the richest, strongest, smartest, most powerful empire in history. You can't imagine a world without it. And Christianity is a small cult based on messianic prophecies and rooted in Judaism. Judaism is dead. You own Jewish slaves. Rome crushed two Jewish revolts. The Jews don't have money, power, or influence. Jewish ideas – in any form – will never overwhelm Roman ideas.

But what happened? By the year 300 the Roman emperor – Constantine the Great – converted to Christianity. The empire converted to Christianity too. The state religion was Christianity. Most of the citizens were Christian. Rome adopted the values, ideals, ethics, and basics of Judaism.[28]

How did that happen? How did the Jews – an oppressed minority – change the religion of the most powerful empire in history?

It doesn't make sense.

Islamic history is similar. Mohamed – Islam's Prophet – was born in Mecca. He was persecuted in Mecca and compelled to leave. In 622, he moved to Yathrib (later renamed Medina). A delegation from Yathrib asked him to act as peacemaker between local tribes and mediate disputes. He ruled Medina, raided Quraishi caravans, won a miraculous victory in Badr, and either killed or expelled leading Jewish clans from Yathrib. In 627, he massacred the Jewish community.

Mohamed made a truce with Mecca's leadership in 628. He used the opportunity to crush the rebellious Jewish communities in nearby Khaibar and Fadak. These Jews were allowed to live, but forced to pay fifty percent of their income to the Muslims. In 630, Mohamed conquered Mecca, consolidated his power, and by the end of his life ruled the Arabian Peninsula.[29]

The Koran does not mandate wanton slaughter of Jews. Jews are allowed to live in Muslim society as *Dhimi* or second-class citizens.

Jews pay a special tax, cannot testify in a Muslim court, and are subject to humiliation and persecution.[30]

But Islam is in debt to the Jews. The Koran maintains much of the Torah's narrative (although it alters significant details). It accepts lineage to Abraham via his son Ishmael. It mandates prayer, charity, dietary laws, and study. It prohibits idolatry. Many Muslims even practice circumcision.

Mohamed invented a religion based on the beliefs of a minority he oppressed. His nation converted to his religion. They oppressed that minority too.

It makes as much sense as Rome becoming Christian.

Think about it. Between the Christians and Muslims, most of the people who oppressed, murdered, persecuted, and tortured Jews over the last 2,000 years practiced a religion based on Jewish ideas. They read the Jewish bible (or a version of it), named their children after the Jewish prophets, and – at least the Christians – worshiped a Jewish man executed for being the Jewish messiah.

Talk about weird.

Forget religion. What about Jews? Are Jewish people influential?

163 out of 750 Nobel Prizes were awarded to Jews (as of 2008).[31] That is about 22%. The Jewish people are only 0.227% of the world's total population: i.e. they are over-represented by about 11,500%.

In the United States, 13 Senators are Jewish. 32 Congressmen are Jewish. Jews are represented in the cabinet, as high-level executive appointments, and on the Supreme Court. Jews run the Fed, major banks on Wall Street, and are CEOs of major companies. Jews own most of the major Hollywood studios (and many actors are Jewish, too).

The only thing Jews don't dominate is sports. Although they own many professional sports teams.

And it gets better. The four thinkers who had the biggest impact on the 20th century were Einstein, Marx, Freud, and Darwin.[32] Three were Jewish. Darwin wasn't. Time Magazine selected Einstein as their Man of the Century.

Jews excel at everything they do. Even the biggest criminals are Jewish. Meyer Lansky, Bugsy Siegel, Ivan Boesky, and Bernie Madoff are Jewish.

John Adams was right. No one has influenced the affairs of mankind more than the Jewish people. Jewish ideas are considered unalienable rights. Jewish people are at the forefront of every field and innovation.

And God promised the Jewish people that they would be influential:

> And I the Lord have called you in righteousness, and I will hold your hand and keep you. And I will establish you as a covenant of the people, for a light unto the nations.[33]

God can deliver.

But if you take God out of the picture, can you explain how the Jews are so disproportionately influential?

6. Return To Israel – and –
7. The Interdependence of the Nation and Land

2,000 years ago, the Land of Israel was a Roman province.

The Roman rulers were oppressive, corrupt, and levied heavy taxes. They issued decrees, outlawed the Jewish religion, razed villages, sold Jews into slavery, destroyed Jewish cities and symbols, and made Israel a dangerous place for Jews to live.

The Jews rebelled in the years 66-70 and again in 132-135. Both revolts were squashed and thousands of Jews were killed.[34]

By the time the last Roman Emperor was deposed in 476, most Jews were in exile – far from the Land of Israel and Roman rule.[35]

And the Jews stayed away. Some Jews remained. Some Jewish communities in Israel flourished from time-to-time. But most Jews lived in the Diaspora.

In the mid-19th century – 1,500 years later – the Jews started to return to Israel *en masse*. A second wave followed. The political Zionist movement – led by Theodore Herzl – was launched in 1897 with the First Zionist Congress. By World War I Israel had a significant Jewish population. The Jewish State declared its independence in 1948 and the population of the new state was about 600,000 people.[36]

In ancient times – from the biblical period through Roman rule – the Land of Israel was an economic goldmine. Historians call it the Fertile Crescent. The bible called it "the land of milk and honey." It was rich from olive oil, dates, spices, grains, wine, and other exports. Major trade routes passed through the region.

The Land of Israel was a region rolling in cash.

How rich was it?

Herod the Great was king of Roman Palestine[37] and a Roman puppet. He was a master builder. He was prolific. He built Caesarea: a grand city with a manmade deep-sea port, aqueduct, hippodrome, and amphitheater.[38] He built Masada: a luxury palace on top of a tall, thin plateau in the desert. He built an enormous shrine over the Cave of the Patriarchs in Hebron. He built Herodium: a manmade mountain fortress.

And he renovated the Temple Complex in Jerusalem. The Temple Complex was built on top of a massive platform. He made the platform by flattening the mountain the Temple Complex was built on. Herod's platform is still the largest manmade platform in the world today.

How did he pay for these ambitious, expensive, large-scale building projects?

Taxes.

Herod had money. The money he collected paid for his buildings. It also paid for his lifestyle, wars, palaces, staff, civil services, a standing army, and the other expenses and trappings of government.

Israel was rich, viable, productive, and prosperous. It was a land that supported opulence and extravagance. And it was rich enough to fund the dreams of an egotistical, megalomaniac like Herod.

What happened?

The Jews fled and the area fell into decline. The Land of Israel was an unproductive, sparsely inhabited wasteland from the end of the Roman period until modern times. Israel is rarely – if ever – mentioned in Byzantine or Arab history (except for the Crusades and the construction of a few Mosques in Jerusalem).[39] Nothing happened in Israel. Very few people lived there. It was unproductive. It wasn't economically viable. It was a backwater in the Ottoman Empire. By the end of the 19th century, three families owned most of the land.[40] Fellahin peasants farmed it; they were poor and oppressed.

This is what Nachmanides, a famous medieval rabbi, said about Israel when he moved there in 1260:

What shall I tell you about the land? There are so many for-
saken places, and the desolation is great. It comes down to this:
the more sacred the place, the more it has suffered – Jerusalem
is most desolate, Judea more so than the Galilee. Yet in all its
desolation it is an exceedingly good land.[41]

Mark Twain went to visit in 1867. Look at what he had to say:

We traversed some miles of desolate country whose soil is
rich enough but is given wholly to weeds - a silent, mournful expanse... A desolation is here that not even imagination
can grace with the pomp of life and action. We reached Tabor
safely... We never saw a human being on the whole route. We
pressed on toward the goal of our crusade, renowned Jerusalem. The further we went the hotter the sun got and the more
rocky and bare, repulsive and dreary the landscape became...
There was hardly a tree or a shrub anywhere. Even the olive and
the cactus, those fast friends of a worthless soil, had almost de-
serted the country. No landscape exists that is more tiresome to
the eye than that which bounds the approaches to Jerusalem...
Jerusalem is mournful, dreary and lifeless. I would not desire to
live here. It is a hopeless, dreary, heartbroken land...Palestine
sits in sackcloth and ashes.[42]

Sounds like he had a terrible time. Weird. Israel was filthy rich in
ancient times. But when the Jews left, it fell into decline.

And then the Jews returned. What happened?

It became prosperous again. In 1997, the International Monetary
Fund took Israel off its list of developing countries. Israel exports
more than it imports. It is a leader in high-tech, biotech, irrigation
technologies, and the list goes on. It has the 19th highest standard of
living in the world (just behind England).[43]

Immigrants flock to Israel. It experienced a 900% increase in
population by 2007. In the first six years of independence, a population of 600,000 absorbed 580,000 immigrants. And absorbing immigrants is expensive.[44]

Does that make sense?

Israel was productive. The Jews left and it was unproductive. The
Jews returned and it was productive again.

Why couldn't anyone make the Land of Israel prosperous when
the Jews were gone? The Jews were away for 1,500 years. 1,500 years

is a long time. No one cared? No one could figure out how to make it work? Why not? Good land is good land. It doesn't matter who lives on it.

The American Great Plains were productive before the Europeans farmed them. They are still productive. The Great Plains didn't weep when the Native Americans were forced off. Land is land. Farming is farming. Land doesn't ask farmers for their passports. Farmers farm and the land produces.

But not the Land of Israel. Its productivity is linked to the population. And it produces when the population is Jewish.

Why is that?

The Torah tells the Jews what will happen to the land when they are exiled:

> So devastated will I leave the land that your enemies who live there will be astonished... Your land will remain desolate, and your cities in ruins.[45]

And the Torah tells the Jews what will happen to the land when they return:

> And the Lord your God shall return you from you your captivity and have compassion upon you; He shall return and gather you from among all the nations... And the Lord your God will bring you into the land that your fathers inherited. You will acquire it, and He will make you even more prosperous and numerous than your fathers.[46]

Odd.

But it happened. Israel is only productive when Jews live there.

Take it a step further. The Jews returned. That is odd, too. Most nations go into exile and disappear. They don't return and rebuild – certainly not 1,500 years later.

Travel back in time. Go back to 1850. Ask a Jew if he could imagine the founding of a Jewish state in the Land of Israel.

No way. Inconceivable.

True, he prayed for it every day. But it was a dream. If you told him it would happen by 1948, he would think you were crazy.

Herzl wrote in his diary that the Jewish state would be founded in fifty years (he died in 1904). He was right. But he only wrote it in his diary. He didn't say it in public. No one would take him seriously if he did.[47]

But it happened. The Jews survived exile. They went home. The State of Israel was declared in 1948. And now more Jews live in Israel than in any Diaspora community.

And the land responded. It bloomed when the Jews came home. Crazy?

Jewish survival is crazy. I said so at the beginning. Nations don't survive the things the Jewish people survived. Look what happened. The Jews were oppressed, scattered, few in number, hated, and despised.

But they survived.

And they didn't just survive; they changed the world. Remember that quote from John Adams? The Jews made a massive contribution to world religion, ethics, and morals. Jewish values are considered unalienable rights. The two biggest religions in the world are based on Judaism.

And what about Jewish people? They are noted in every field, business, discipline, craft, innovation, and area you can think of.

The Jews went home. And their land waited for them to return. After a 1,500-year break, the Land of Israel is prosperous like it was in ancient times.

How do you explain these things?

Think about one more thing. The contradictory, insane, unusual, unique history of the Jewish people was written in the Torah – at least 2,000 years ago – before any of it happened. The Torah was explicit. It warned the Jewish people about their destiny in clear, unambiguous language. And the claims were made at the start of Jewish history. Before the Jews did anything.

And the Torah was right. The claims and contradictions happened the way it said they would.

How do you explain that?

You have to decide.

Did a lunatic write the Torah? Who made the crazy, contradictory, anomalous claims about the future and wrote them down? Was he a madman? Is the Torah a wild guess?

Maybe. But how did he get it right? And if he was crazy, how do you explain the rest of the Torah? The rest of the Torah is very sensible.

Maybe a committee of enlightened sages wrote the Torah.

Maybe. But I doubt it. I don't think intelligent people would make unusual predictions that are unlikely to come true – certainly not seven contradictory predictions – it would destroy their credibility. And no one would trust the rest of the book.

Or maybe God wrote the Torah.

Does that bother you?

Why?

It makes sense. God controls history. God knows the future. God can predict seven contradictions if He wants to. He can guarantee they work out.

And the Torah claims God wrote it.

Think about it. It doesn't make sense to include seven crazy, contradictory predictions in the Torah. They don't add anything to the story. They detract if they don't work out. No sane person would add them.

But what if you knew they would occur? Would you add them? It is powerful to make predictions that come true – especially seven unusual, contradictory, unique, anomalous predictions about a small, scattered, hated, but influential nation.

God knows the future. He can make explicit predictions. He isn't afraid of the consequences. It makes sense for Him to include them in His book. Seven unusual, explicit, contradictory predictions are a great tool for future generations.

And including these predictions – especially when they come true – is evidence that He wrote the Torah.

Think about it. What are the other options? Did a lunatic or a committee of sages write the Torah? Did it evolve? Was it a lucky guess?

Or does it make more sense to say that God wrote it?

You Do the Math

The Story of the Torah Codes

P retend your name is Mike.

One morning, as you are eating breakfast, you try to see if your name is encoded in the newspaper. You find a letter M. From M you start counting letters. Fifty letters after M you find I. Impressive. You count another fifty letters, K. And fifty letters after K, you find E. Amazing. Your name, Mike, is encoded in the newspaper at an interval of every fifty letters.

Yikes.

How did it get there? Maybe God wrote the newspaper.

But why did you count letters in the newspaper in the first place? It is a weird thing to do.

How about the Torah?

Are names, dates, places, and events hidden in the text of the Torah? Maybe. But why look there? It is a strange idea. Why suspect the Torah contains hidden information?

According to Jewish tradition, the Torah is a set of instructions. But it is more than that. Take a look at this quote from the Zohar, the primary work of Jewish mysticism:

> God looked into the Torah and created the world.

That is an unusual thing to say. It implies that God used the Torah as a blueprint for creation.

Interesting.

A blueprint contains every detail. Your house was built based on a design drawn by an architect. Every electrical outlet, heating vent, corner, closet, door, window, pipe, and rafter was included in that drawing. The carpenters, electricians, plumbers, and roofers used it to build your house.

What details are contained in the Torah, the blueprint for creation?

Look at this quote from the Vilna Gaon. The Vilna Gaon's real name was Rabbi Eliyahu from Vilna. He died in 1797 and was one of the most influential rabbis of the last 300 years. He was a genius. And he was a prolific author. This is what he said about the Torah being a blueprint:

> The rule is that all that was, is, and will be until the end of time is included in the Torah from the first verse in Genesis until that last word in Deuteronomy. And not merely in a general sense – but including the details of every species and of each person individually – and the most minute details of everything that happened to him – from the day of his birth until his death.[48]

Think about it. According to the Vilna Gaon, everything is in the blueprint: every tree, every flower, every rock, every person, and every experience. Nothing is missing. World War Two is in the blueprint. What you ate for breakfast is in the blueprint. Everything is in there.

That is a very big claim.

How do you find every minute detail in the Torah? It isn't a big book. How does it contain every detail in history?

Look at this quote from Rabbi Moshe Cordovero. Rabbi Cordovero was a leading rabbi from Tzfat. He was the head of the Jewish court there. And he was one of the most important writers of Jewish mysticism. This quote is from his first major work, the *Pardes Rimonim*, written in 1542.

> The secrets of our holy Torah are revealed through knowledge of combinations, numerology (*gematria*), switching letters, first-and-last letters, shapes of letters, first-and-last verses, *skipping*

letters, and letter combinations. These matters are powerful, hidden, and enormous secrets. Because they are so well hidden, we don't have the ability to fully comprehend them. Furthermore, to see different angles through these methods is infinite and without limit. On this the Torah says, "Its measure is longer than the world."[49]

In other words, every detail is in the Torah. You can find it if you know how to look. Rabbi Cordovero listed a number of different tools. One of those tools was skipping letters. Theoretically, if you skip through sequences of letters in the original Hebrew version of the Torah you will find hidden information.[50]

Take a look.

Rabbi Chaim Michael Dov Weissmandl was the head of a yeshiva in Czechoslovakia.[51] During the Holocaust, he tried to raise money to bribe Nazi officials. He met with Nazi leaders in secret and made deals to free Jews. He sent letters to the Pope, Winston Churchill, and FDR. He begged the Allies to bomb Auschwitz.

That is what he is famous for.

But he was also a great Torah scholar. He wrote commentaries, essays, and discussions of Jewish law. He also wrote about his study of equidistant letter skips in the Torah.

What is an equidistant letter skip?

Pick a word. Find the first letter in the Torah. Count until you find the next letter. Don't count blank spaces or punctuation. Count from the second letter until you find the third. Is the distance between the first and second letter the same as that between the second and third? How about from the third to the forth?

That is an equidistant letter skip.

Rabbi Weissmandl wrote Biblical verses on index cards in grids of ten letters by ten letters. He omitted the spaces. He studied the grids. He found words hidden at equidistant intervals. And many of his findings were significant.

After his death in 1957, his students published a collection of his writings. The collection was called *Toras Chemed*. In addition to his commentaries and essays, *Toras Chemed* included his work with equidistant letter skips.

Here is an example.

Look at the first verse in the Torah. Do you know it?

"In the beginning, God created the heaven and the earth."

In Hebrew, the last letter of the first word is Tav. A Tav looks like this: ת. Tav is also the first letter in the word, "Torah." Look at the quote below in Hebrew. Count fifty letters from that first Tav. The second letter you reach is Vav, ו. Fifty letters later is Reish, ר. And fifty letters after that is Hey, ה. That spells the word, "Torah." "Torah" is encoded from the beginning of the Torah, from the first appearance of a Tav, at an equidistant letter skip of fifty.[52]

See it for yourself. I circled the letters to make it easy to find.

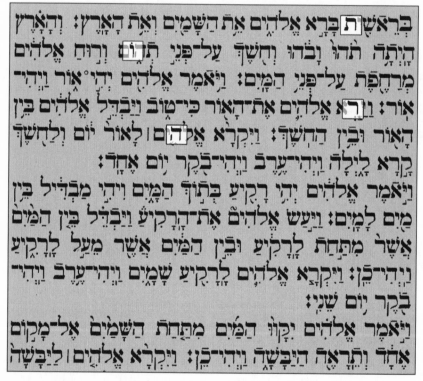

Figure 1.

Interesting.
Does it prove anything? No. Is it significant? Maybe.
Or maybe not.
If you found the word, "Times," at an equidistant letter skip of fifty on the first page of the New York Times, you would con-

clude one of two things: either it was random, or someone put it there.

And in your mind, the chances of either are equally plausible.

But if you found the word "Times" the next day at an equidistant letter skip of fifty, the chance of it being random is less likely. If the phenomena happened again the next day, and again the day after that, by the end of the week you would conclude that someone did it on purpose. It is unlikely that a specific idea – like the appearance of the newspaper's name at an equidistant skip of fifty letters – appeared by chance on the front page every day for a week.

It isn't impossible. But it is unlikely.

The Torah is called the Five Books of Moses. It is a five-volume set. The first book is the Book of Genesis. The word "Torah" appears at an equidistant skip of fifty letters at the beginning of the Book of Genesis. How about the next book?

The second book is the Book of Exodus. Tav is the last letter of the second word. Count fifty letters from the first Tav. The next letter you reach is Vav. Keep counting. The next letter is Reish and the next letter after that is Hey.

It happened again.

"Torah" is encoded at an equidistant skip of fifty letters at the beginning of the second book, too.

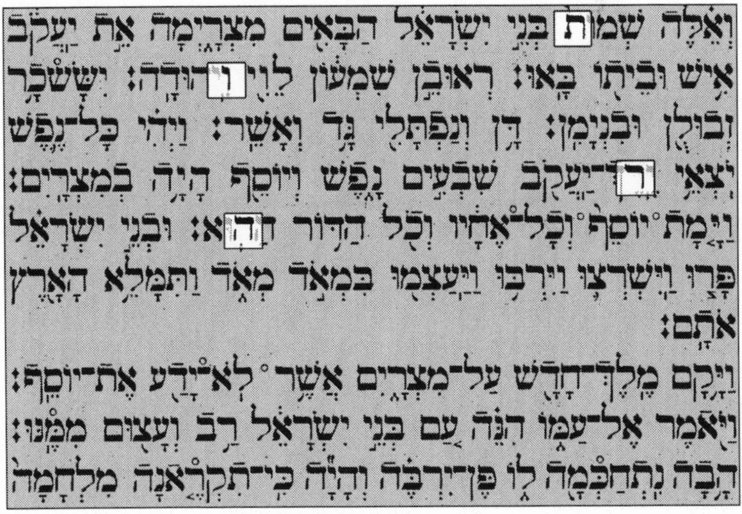
ואלה שמות בני ישראל הבאים מצרימה את יעקב
איש וביתו באו: ראובן שמעון לוי ויהודה: יששכר
זבולן ובנימן: דן ונפתלי גד ואשר: ויהי כל־נפש
יצאי ירך־יעקב שבעים נפש ויוסף היה במצרים:
וימת יוסף וכל־אחיו וכל הדור ההוא: ובני ישראל
פרו וישרצו וירבו ויעצמו במאד מאד ותמלא הארץ
אתם:
ויקם מלך־חדש על־מצרים אשר לא־ידע את־יוסף:
ויאמר אל־עמו הנה עם בני ישראל רב ועצום ממנו:
הבה נתחכמה לו פן־ירבה והיה כי־תקראנה מלחמה

Figure 2.

Is it a random occurrence? Maybe. But it is less likely to be random than if it only happened once.

Look at the next book. The third book is the Book of Leviticus. Find the first Tav. Count fifty letters. Keep counting.

Nothing.

"Torah" is not encoded at the beginning of the Book of Leviticus at an equidistant letter skip of fifty. It isn't encoded at the beginning of the book at all.

Are you disappointed?

Are you relieved?

Look at the next book. The fourth book is the Book of Numbers. "Torah" is there, at the beginning, and at an equidistant letter skip of fifty. But it is backwards. Take a look:

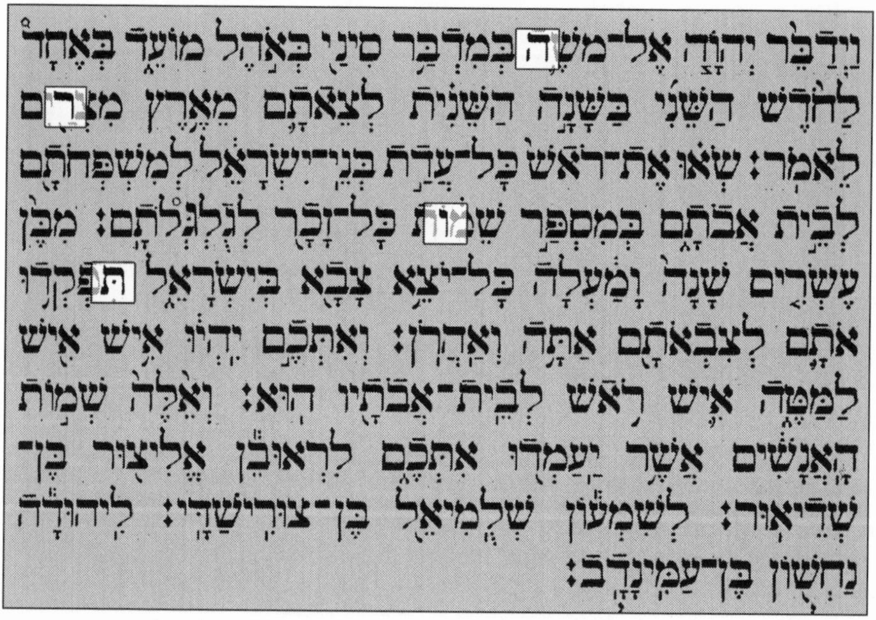
וידבר יהוה אל־משה במדבר סיני באהל מועד באחד
לחדש השני בשנה השנית לצאתם מארץ מצרים
לאמר׃ שאו את־ראש כל־עדת בני־ישראל למשפחתם
לבית אבתם במספר שמות כל־זכר לגלגלתם׃ מבן
עשרים שנה ומעלה כל־יצא צבא בישראל תפקדו
אתם לצבאתם אתה ואהרן׃ ואתכם יהיו איש איש
למטה איש ראש לבית־אבתיו הוא׃ ואלה שמות
האנשים אשר יעמדו אתכם לראובן אליצור בן
שדיאור׃ לשמעון שלמיאל בן־צורישדי׃ ליהודה
נחשון בן־עמינדב׃

Figure 3.

Also notice, the first letter in the backwards sequence – Hey – is not the first Hey in the book.

Significant? Maybe. But not as impressive as finding "Times" everyday for a week on the front page of the paper.

Look at the last book. The fifth book is the Book of Deuteronomy. "Torah" is there. And it is backwards again, too. But it is at an equidistant skip of forty-nine, not fifty. And it doesn't start at the beginning; it is a few verses into the book.

Impressed?

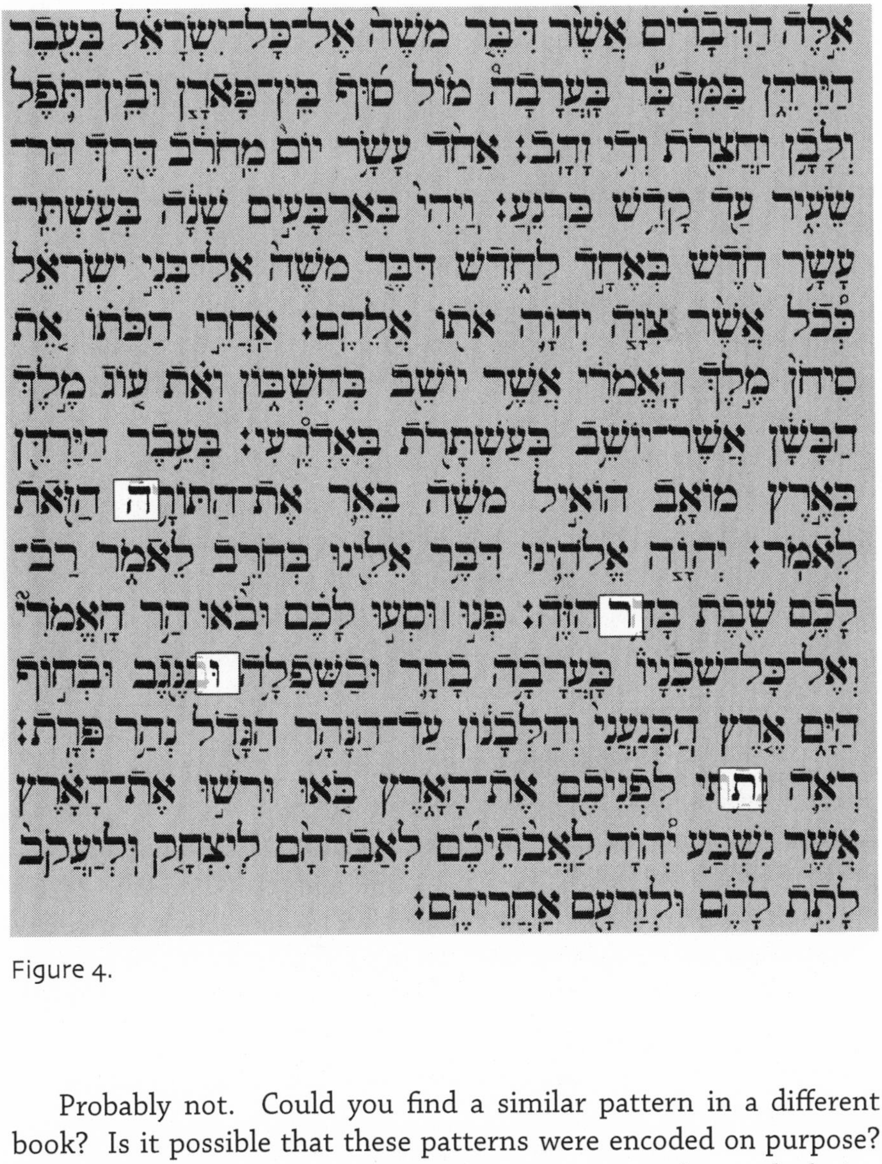

אֵלֶּה הַדְּבָרִים אֲשֶׁר דִּבֶּר מֹשֶׁה אֶל־כָּל־יִשְׂרָאֵל בְּעֵבֶר
הַיַּרְדֵּן בַּמִּדְבָּר בָּעֲרָבָה מוֹל סוּף בֵּין־פָּארָן וּבֵין־תֹּפֶל
וְלָבָן וַחֲצֵרֹת וְדִי זָהָב׃ אַחַד עָשָׂר יוֹם מֵחֹרֵב דֶּרֶךְ הַר־
שֵׂעִיר עַד קָדֵשׁ בַּרְנֵעַ׃ וַיְהִי בְּאַרְבָּעִים שָׁנָה בְּעַשְׁתֵּי־
עָשָׂר חֹדֶשׁ בְּאֶחָד לַחֹדֶשׁ דִּבֶּר מֹשֶׁה אֶל־בְּנֵי יִשְׂרָאֵל
כְּכֹל אֲשֶׁר צִוָּה יְהוָה אֹתוֹ אֲלֵהֶם׃ אַחֲרֵי הַכֹּתוֹ אֵת
סִיחֹן מֶלֶךְ הָאֱמֹרִי אֲשֶׁר יוֹשֵׁב בְּחֶשְׁבּוֹן וְאֵת עוֹג מֶלֶךְ
הַבָּשָׁן אֲשֶׁר־יוֹשֵׁב בְּעַשְׁתָּרֹת בְּאֶדְרֶעִי׃ בְּעֵבֶר הַיַּרְדֵּן
בְּאֶרֶץ מוֹאָב הוֹאִיל מֹשֶׁה בֵּאֵר אֶת־הַתּוֹרָ[ה] הַזֹּאת
לֵאמֹר׃ יְהוָה אֱלֹהֵינוּ דִּבֶּר אֵלֵינוּ בְּחֹרֵב לֵאמֹר רַב־
לָכֶם שֶׁבֶת בָּ[הָ]ר הַזֶּה׃ פְּנוּ וּסְעוּ לָכֶם וּבֹאוּ הַר הָאֱמֹרִי
וְאֶל־כָּל־שְׁכֵנָיו בָּעֲרָבָה בָהָר וּבַשְּׁפֵלָ[ה] וּבַנֶּגֶב וּבְחוֹף
הַיָּם אֶרֶץ הַכְּנַעֲנִי וְהַלְּבָנוֹן עַד־הַנָּהָר הַגָּדֹל נְהַר־פְּרָת׃
רְאֵה נָ[ת]תִּי לִפְנֵיכֶם אֶת־הָאָרֶץ בֹּאוּ וּרְשׁוּ אֶת־הָאָרֶץ
אֲשֶׁר נִשְׁבַּע יְהוָה לַאֲבֹתֵיכֶם לְאַבְרָהָם לְיִצְחָק וּלְיַעֲקֹב
לָתֵת לָהֶם וּלְזַרְעָם אַחֲרֵיהֶם׃

Figure 4.

Probably not. Could you find a similar pattern in a different book? Is it possible that these patterns were encoded on purpose? Maybe. And these are interesting questions. But without calculating the probability of it happening by accident, it is hard to answer intelligently.

Rabbi Weissmandl was not a scientist or a mathematician or a statistician. He didn't conduct an experiment or calculate probabilities. Rabbi Weissmandl was a Talmudic scholar. His interest in equidistant letter skips was spiritual. He found a number of interesting skips. He recorded them in his notebooks. And his students published his findings after he died.

In the late 1970s, Eliyahu Rips – a professor at Hebrew University in Jerusalem – was impressed with Rabbi Weissmandl's findings. Rips was from Latvia. He was a mathematician. In 1970 he was imprisoned for protesting the Soviet invasion of Czechoslovakia. He was freed in 1972, moved to Israel, finished his PhD, and joined Hebrew University's math department.[53]

Someone showed Rips the equidistant letter skips in Rabbi Weissmandl's book *Toras Chemed*. Interesting. Someone else showed him more sophisticated findings.[54] He was intrigued. He looked for things on his own. He found patterns, clusters, and repeated sequences. Some of his findings were complex, interesting, and statistically significant.[55]

And unlike Rabbi Weissmandl, Rips used a computer.

In the early 1980s, Rips began working with Doron Witztum. Witztum had degrees in math and physics from Hebrew University and started a PhD before leaving to pursue religious studies. Rips and Witztum developed a formal system to examine equidistant letter sequences and to test whether or not the sequences occurred by chance.[56] Based on their calculations, they were convinced that equidistant letter skips in the Torah were not an accident; the mathematical data indicated that they were written into the Torah by design. Someone put them in the Torah on purpose.

But did that someone have to be God?

Not necessarily. You don't need to be God to hide codes in the text of the Torah. You don't need to be God to encode information in any text. Rabbinic literature is full of examples.

Look at Hebrew poetry. In particular, look at the songs sung on Shabbos or the liturgical prayers read on holidays. The first letter of each stanza often spells the poet's name.[57] That is a manmade code.

Jewish writers encoded words in their books as well. For example, the name of God is hidden at the beginning of many important works of law and philosophy.[58] Those are also manmade codes.

Creating equidistant letter skips is easy to do.

The Jewish people wandered in the desert for forty years. They had a lot of free time. It is possible that they played around with the text, moved words, inserted synonyms, and did other tricks in order to encode words at equidistant skips.

Can you think of an equidistant letter skip that cannot be manmade?

How about the future? If you found an equidistant letter skip about a person or event from a period after the Torah was written, you can't say the Jewish people knew about it when they wandered in the desert.

What is considered the future? As I mentioned in the last chapter, according to Jewish tradition, the Torah is about 3,300 years old. The Jewish people gathered at Mount Sinai in 1313 BCE.[59] God spoke to them and gave them the Torah at that time.

If you don't trust Jewish tradition, you still have to say the Torah is old. The Septuagint – the Greek translation of the Torah – was completed about 2,300 years ago.[60] A more recent date is the advent of Christianity. That was about 2,000 years ago. But it is difficult to claim that the Torah is more recent than that.

Look at the next example. It is an equidistant letter skip about Maimonides. Maimonides was an important rabbi. And he lived many years after the most recent date you can assign to the Torah.

Maimonides was born in Cordoba, Spain in 1135. His family feared Islamic persecution and they fled Cordoba when he was a teenager. He spent a few years in Fez, Morocco.

But he spent most of his adult life in Egypt. He was the leading rabbi of his generation. He was a famous doctor as well and was the court physician to Saladin, the great Arab leader. He wrote a number of important works. His most important work was the *Mishna Torah*, a fourteen-volume encyclopedia of Jewish law based on a careful analysis of the 613 commandments. He died in 1204.

"Maimonides" is a Greek version of his name. It means, "Son of Maimon." In Hebrew, his name is Rabbi Moshe ben Maimon. He is commonly referred to as the RAMBAM. RAMBAM is an acronym of Rabbi Moshe ben Maimon. RAMBAM looks like this in Hebrew:

- ℵ Reish – ר
- ℵ Mem – מ
- ℵ Beis – ב
- ℵ Mem – מ[61]

Maimonides died in 1204. He was alive during the Third Crusade. The Torah was an old book at that time. It was already translated into many languages. Christians and Muslims accepted it as authentic.

Anyone who may have inserted equidistant letter skips into the text was long dead by then.

Look at the example below. It is from the Book of Exodus, Chapter 11. In the text, God tells Moses about the Plague of the Firstborn. He tells Moses about the special Passover sacrifice and how to prepare for the Exodus. In verse nine, God tells Moses, "Pharaoh will not listen to you, so that my wonders will be multiplied in the land of Egypt."

Look at the Hebrew text of, "My wonders will be multiplied in the land of Egypt." The first letters spell out RAMBAM. I circled the letters to make it easy to see:

Figure 5.

Interesting. But not a big deal. The Torah is about 80,000 words long. The Hebrew alphabet only has twenty-two letters. It is likely that the first letters of four consecutive words spell RAMBAM in many places. Right?

Wrong.

Scan the entire Torah with a computer. This verse is the only place in the Torah where the first letter of four consecutive words spells RAMBAM.

Interesting.

Maimonides spent most of his adult life in Egypt. What is this verse about? The wonders that will come out of Egypt.

This section is about the Passover sacrifice. The Passover sacrifice was offered on the 14th of the Hebrew month of Nissan. The text says so. And Maimonides' birthday was the 14th of Nissan.

Coincidence?

Maybe. What happens when you look for an equidistant letter skip in this section? Look for Maimonides' most famous work, the Mishna Torah (see Figure 6). The Mishna Torah is a careful analysis of the 613 commandments. It is spelled like this in Hebrew:

משנה תורה ‏א

Do you see it? "Mishna Torah" is hidden in the text at an equidistant letter skip of fifty. And it is hidden near the only verse in the Torah where the first letter of four consecutive words spells RAMBAM.

But what about the gap?

Do you see the huge gap between the end of the word Mishna and the beginning of the word Torah? Count from the first letter of Mishna to the first letter of Torah.

It is 613 letters.

Amazing. Maimonides' name appears only once in the Torah. It appears in a section that talks about Egypt, the place he lived for most of his life. It mentions his birthday. His most famous work is encoded as an equidistant letter skip of fifty. And the break in the skip hints to the subject of his work: the 613 commandments.

How do you explain that? Was it an accident or design? It is hard to say that it was human design. The Torah was written at least 1,100 years before Maimonides was born.

The Maimonides Code is impressive, but it isn't scientific. It doesn't follow the rules of good science. In science, you do three things. You make a hypothesis, i.e. you state, in writing, what you expect will happen. You run the experiment. And then you run a control experiment to make sure your results weren't a fluke. The Maimonides Code was interesting, but it was a lucky guess.

They tried another test[62] and they stated in advance what they were looking for: words related to Chanukah. That was the hypothesis and they limited their search to the Book of Genesis.[63]

וַיֹּאמֶר יְהוָה אֶל־מֹשֶׁה
לֹא־יִשְׁמַע אֲלֵיכֶם פַּרְעֹה לְמַעַן רְבוֹת מוֹפְתַי בְּאֶרֶץ
מִצְרָיִם: וּמֹשֶׁה וְאַהֲרֹן עָשׂוּ אֶת־כָּל־הַמֹּפְתִים הָאֵלֶּה
לִפְנֵי פַרְעֹה וַיְחַזֵּק יְהוָה אֶת־לֵב פַּרְעֹה וְלֹא־שִׁלַּח אֶת־
בְּנֵי־יִשְׂרָאֵל מֵאַרְצוֹ: וַיֹּאמֶר יְהוָה
אֶל־מֹשֶׁה וְאֶל־אַהֲרֹן בְּאֶרֶץ מִצְרַיִם לֵאמֹר: הַחֹדֶשׁ הַזֶּה
לָכֶם רֹאשׁ חֳדָשִׁים רִאשׁוֹן הוּא לָכֶם לְחָדְשֵׁי הַשָּׁנָה:
דַּבְּרוּ אֶל־כָּל־עֲדַת יִשְׂרָאֵל לֵאמֹר בֶּעָשֹׂר לַחֹדֶשׁ הַזֶּה
וְיִקְחוּ לָהֶם אִישׁ שֶׂה לְבֵית־אָבֹת שֶׂה לַבָּיִת: וְאִם־
יִמְעַט הַבַּיִת מִהְיוֹת מִשֶּׂה וְלָקַח הוּא וּשְׁכֵנוֹ הַקָּרֹב אֶל־
בֵּיתוֹ בְּמִכְסַת נְפָשֹׁת אִישׁ לְפִי אָכְלוֹ תָּכֹסּוּ עַל־הַשֶּׂה:
שֶׂה תָמִים זָכָר בֶּן־שָׁנָה יִהְיֶה לָכֶם מִן־הַכְּבָשִׂים וּמִן־
הָעִזִּים תִּקָּחוּ: וְהָיָה לָכֶם לְמִשְׁמֶרֶת עַד אַרְבָּעָה עָשָׂר
יוֹם לַחֹדֶשׁ הַזֶּה וְשָׁחֲטוּ אֹתוֹ כֹּל קְהַל עֲדַת־יִשְׂרָאֵל בֵּין
הָעַרְבָּיִם: וְלָקְחוּ מִן־הַדָּם וְנָתְנוּ עַל־שְׁתֵּי הַמְּזוּזֹת וְעַל־
הַמַּשְׁקוֹף עַל הַבָּתִּים אֲשֶׁר־יֹאכְלוּ אֹתוֹ בָּהֶם: וְאָכְלוּ
אֶת־הַבָּשָׂר בַּלַּיְלָה הַזֶּה צְלִי־אֵשׁ וּמַצּוֹת עַל־מְרֹרִים
יֹאכְלֻהוּ: אַל־תֹּאכְלוּ מִמֶּנּוּ נָא וּבָשֵׁל מְבֻשָּׁל בַּמָּיִם כִּי
אִם־צְלִי־אֵשׁ רֹאשׁוֹ עַל־כְּרָעָיו וְעַל־קִרְבּוֹ: וְלֹא־תוֹתִירוּ
מִמֶּנּוּ עַד־בֹּקֶר וְהַנֹּתָר מִמֶּנּוּ עַד־בֹּקֶר בָּאֵשׁ תִּשְׂרֹפוּ:
וְכָכָה תֹּאכְלוּ אֹתוֹ מָתְנֵיכֶם חֲגֻרִים נַעֲלֵיכֶם בְּרַגְלֵיכֶם
וּמַקֶּלְכֶם בְּיֶדְכֶם וַאֲכַלְתֶּם אֹתוֹ בְּחִפָּזוֹן פֶּסַח הוּא
לַיהוָה: וְעָבַרְתִּי בְאֶרֶץ־מִצְרַיִם בַּלַּיְלָה הַזֶּה וְהִכֵּיתִי
כָל־בְּכוֹר בְּאֶרֶץ מִצְרַיִם מֵאָדָם וְעַד־בְּהֵמָה וּבְכָל־
אֱלֹהֵי מִצְרַיִם אֶעֱשֶׂה שְׁפָטִים אֲנִי יְהוָה: וְהָיָה הַדָּם
לָכֶם לְאֹת עַל הַבָּתִּים אֲשֶׁר אַתֶּם שָׁם וְרָאִיתִי אֶת־
הַדָּם וּפָסַחְתִּי עֲלֵכֶם וְלֹא־יִהְיֶה בָכֶם נֶגֶף לְמַשְׁחִית
בְּהַכֹּתִי בְּאֶרֶץ מִצְרָיִם:

Figure 6.

Look at what they found.

The computer found "Chanukah" in the Book of Genesis at an equidistant letter skip of 262 (backwards). 262 was the minimal skip.

What is a minimal skip?

If you search for the word "Chanukah," you may find it more than once. It may exist at a skip of every 500 letters or every 10,000 letters. But 262 is the minimum. It means you won't find "Chanukah" in the Book of Genesis at a skip less than 262.[64]

Was it interesting that they found "Chanukah" in the Book of Genesis? Yes. Was it significant? Not really. The Book of Genesis is a big book. If you look hard enough, and you skip enough letters, you can find any word you want.

What made the experiment significant?

The experiment was significant because a) they found other words related to Chanukah and b) they found them in the same part of the text.

Pretend that you and I are sitting in Yankee Stadium. We are alone in the stadium. We are sitting in the top rows, far away from the field. I throw a paper airplane. It floats through the air, swoops up and down, and lands on home plate.

Amazing. But I probably got lucky.

I make another paper airplane. Same thing, it also lands on home plate. How did I do it?

I make a few more paper airplanes; they land on home plate too.

Yikes. One plane landing on home plate was a fluke. But all of them?

You don't know how I did it. But you know that I did something. Maybe I studied the wind currents in the stadium. Maybe I installed a giant magnet under home plate. I certainly didn't get lucky each time.

Look at the next example.

The heroes in the Chanukah story were the Hasmoneans. The family name was Hasmonean. In Hebrew it was Chashmonyi. Look at the example. The computer found Chasmonyi right next to the word "Chanukah" and at a minimal skip of 525 letters.

Chanukah	החנוכה
Hasmonean	חשממונאי
Maccabee	מכבי
Judah	יהודה
Greece	יון
8 Days	ח ימים

Figure 7.

The Book of Genesis is about 78,000 letters long. Chashmonyi could have been anywhere. It turned up right next to Chanukah. It is as if I threw the second paper airplane and it landed on home plate, right next to the first one.

Maccabee is another Chanukah word. Maccabee was the name of the Hasmonean's army. The computer found Maccabee at a minimal skip of two. And it found it right on top of Chanukah.

Judah was the leader of the Maccabees. In Hebrew, Judah is Yehudah. Yehudah is in the text, in the same place as the other words.

The battle at the time of Chanukah was against the Greeks. Greece is Yavan in Hebrew. The computer found "Yavan" backwards and at a minimal skip of one. And it found it intersecting the word "Chashmonyi."

The Chanukah miracle lasted eight days. "Ches Yamim" is the way to write eight days in Hebrew. "Ches Yamim" is also at a skip of 262 letters and in the same area as the other words.

That is a code. And it is amazing. Every paper airplane landed on home plate. What happened?

I want to be clear. You will find words – or codes[65] – in any large text you study. You will find codes in the newspaper, a novel, the New Testament, a comic book, or on the back of a box of cereal. Finding a code is not impressive. What is impressive? Finding groups of related words encoded and clustered in the same area in the same text. I am not interested in finding words. I am interested in groups of related words. That is a code. Anything else is silly.

Here is another example.

Hypothesis: look for words related to diabetes. Diabetes in Hebrew is *sakeret*.

The computer found "*sakeret*" in the Book of Genesis at a minimal equidistant skip of six. Interesting. The computer looked for more words. It found "*lavlav*," the Hebrew word for pancreas. Diabetes affects the pancreas. "*Lavlav*" is in the same part of the text as "*sakeret*." Very interesting. The computer found one more word: Insulin. Insulin is a hormone. Diabetes is the result of the body's inability to produce or regulate insulin.[66] The equidistant letter skip of "insulin" is huge, 3,378 letters, but it is the shortest skip of "insulin" in the Book of Genesis. And it lands right between "*sakeret*" and "*lavlav*." Amazing.

Take a look (see Figure 8).

Impressive. Insulin was not used in the treatment of diabetes until 1921 and synthetic insulin was not produced until the 1960s.[67] It was impossible to believe that the Jews encoded "insulin" into the

Pancreas   לבלב

Diabetes   סכרת

Insulin   אנסולין

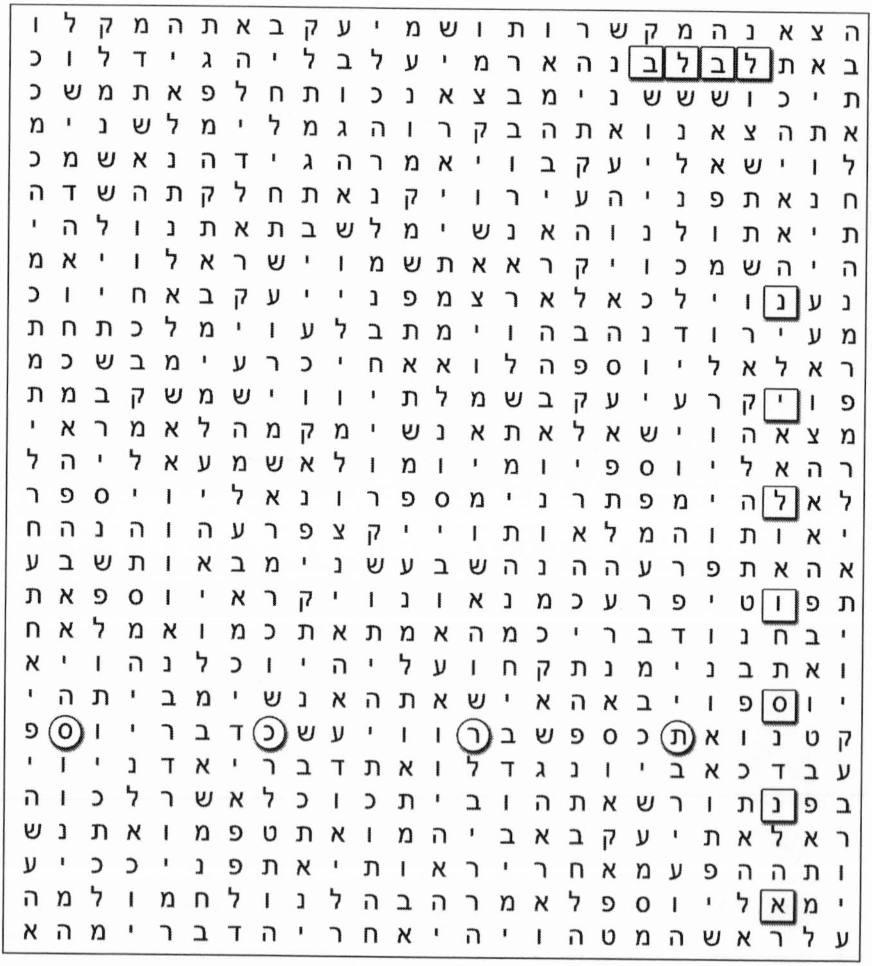

Figure 8.

text in 1313 BCE, when they were wandering in the desert. Rips and Witztum decided to get their data published in a journal of statistics. The findings were serious.[68]

Rips and Witztum took their data to *Statistical Science: a review journal of the institute of mathematical statistics*.[69] Statistical Science is one of the top journals of statistics in the world. It is the kind of journal found in university libraries and science departments. People who love math read it. Statistical Science was not impressed. "We think you cheated," they told Rips and Witztum.

Is it possible to cheat? Yes. Go back to the paper airplane example. You and I are sitting alone in Yankee Stadium. I make a paper airplane. You leave to go to the bathroom. While you are away, I throw 30,000 paper airplanes down to the field. They land everywhere. I call the ground crew and ask them to sweep up all the airplanes, except for the five or six planes that landed on home plate. You return. I point to the airplanes on home plate. "Look at what I did. I threw a few planes and they all landed on home plate. I am a genius."

Are you impressed? Not at all.

That is called a hidden failure. I show you my successes. I don't show you my failures.

The journal said to Rips and Witztum, "How do we know you didn't look for *every* Jewish holiday? How do we know you didn't look for thousands of words related to each holiday? How do we know you didn't look for thousands of diseases? You got lucky with the Chanukah and Diabetes examples. But you cheated. You didn't show us your thousands of failed attempts."

They had a point.

Rips and Witztum met with the editorial board of Statistical Science. They proposed an experiment. They created a list of famous rabbis. The list included each rabbi's name[70] and the dates of his birth and death. They agreed to:

  a. Find the rabbi's name as an equidistant letter skip
  b. Find the rabbi's dates of birth and death as an equidistant letter skip
  c. Determine if the rabbi's name and dates were in close proximity to each other. (The concept of "close" was defined in a precise mathematical way.)[71]

The original list of rabbis was taken from the *Encyclopedia of Great Men in Israel*. Thirty-four names were chosen (specifically, the list included any rabbi who had at least three columns of text written about him in the encyclopedia[72]). Professor Shlomo Havlin – head of the Department of Bibliography and Librarianship at Bar Ilan University – prepared the list. A linguist, Dr. Yaakov Orbach, established the rules of orthography and the form of the Hebrew date.

The results looked very successful.[73] Look at this example (see Figure 9).

Rabbi Shlomo Luria was born in 1510 and died in 1574. He was a leading rabbi in Poland and Lithuania. And he wrote a number of important commentaries on the Talmud. He was known as the Maharshal, a Hebrew acronym that stands for Our Teacher, Rabbi Shlomo Luria. The Hebrew date of his death was the 12th of the Hebrew month of Kislev.

The computer found his name, the Maharshal (HaMaharshal), at a minimum equidistant letter skip of 229. His date of death, the 12th of Kislev, was found at a minimum skip of 114. The computer found the year he died, 5334, at a backwards skip of two. And it found his name, Shlomo, at a backwards skip of two as well.

Take a look. Notice the close proximity of each of the findings.

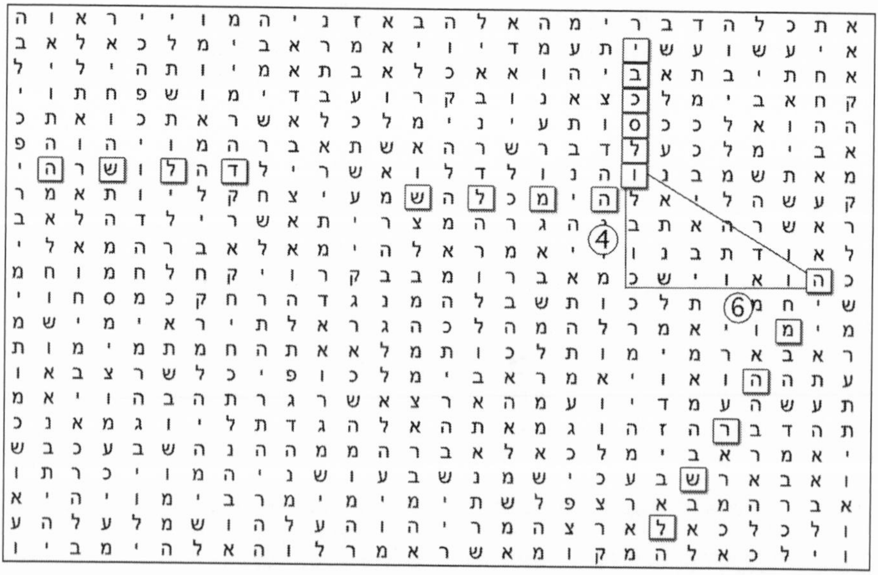

Figure 9.

HaMaharshal	המהרשל
Shlomo	המלש
12 Kislev	יב כסלו
5334	השלד

$$\sqrt{6^2 + 4^2} = \sqrt{52} = 7.21 \text{ (Fancy math noted in Figure 9.)}$$

The experiment for Statistical Science was only concerned with the rabbi's name and dates of birth and death. Calculate the proximity. Draw a triangle. Do fancy math. The linear distance between the name and date is 7.21 letters. That looks like a success.

Not every name and date was as close as the Maharshal. Some had a linear distance of twenty letters. Some had a linear distance of fifty letters. Some didn't work. But enough examples worked, and enough examples were close, that Statistical Science was impressed and decided to publish.

But they were chicken.

The journal sent a letter to Rips and Witztum. The experiment was too controversial. They changed their mind. They were not going to publish it.

Not fair. If the science was bunk, fine. But if the science was good, how could the journal back out? Statistical Science argued that their reputation was on the line. Even if the science was good, the conclusions sounded like hocus-pocus. If someone found a mistake, it would destroy the journal's credibility.[74]

But they agreed to a compromise. If the world's leading statistician validated the results – and signed his name – they would publish the paper.

The statistician they favored was Professor Persi Diaconis.

Professor Diaconis was an interesting character. He had a Ph.D. from Harvard in Mathematical Statistics. He was a leading professor at Stanford. He was a magician. He won the prestigious MacArthur Fellowship – a $500,000 genius grant given to recipients to spend as they please – for his work calculating the level of randomness in a shuffled deck of cards.[75] He had a reputation as a debunker. In the mid-1970s, he exposed key problems in ESP research and debunked a handful of famed psychics.[76] He was a skeptic.

If Diaconis said the equidistant letter skip research was legit, the journal would publish the paper. Otherwise, forget it.

Rips and Witztum contacted Diaconis. They sent him a copy of the paper they prepared for publication. Diaconis suggested they re-run the experiment with a new list of rabbis. A new list of thirty-two names was chosen from the *Encyclopedia of Great Men in Israel*. (The new list was made up of rabbis' names with between one-and-a-half and three columns of text written about them in the encyclopedia.[77]) Professor Havlin prepared this list as well. The experiment was run and the results were similar to the first.

Diaconis wanted control experiments run as well. Rips and Witztum searched for equidistant letter skips in other books (including the Samaritan Torah[78] and versions of Genesis with the words and sentences jumbled). They looked for the rabbi's names in close proximity to their dates of birth and death. These books – the books used as control experiments – were about the same length as the Book of Genesis.

They searched a Hebrew translation of *War and Peace*.[79] Nothing. They searched a Hebrew translation of *Moby Dick*. Nothing. They looked in modern Israeli novels. Nothing. They looked in ancient Hebrew books. Nothing. They searched tens of examples. Nothing had as many multiple equidistant letter skips in close proximity as did the Book of Genesis.

Diaconis wanted more tests. Robert Aumann, a professor at Hebrew University and the 2005 winner of the Nobel Prize in Economics, negotiated a deal. Rips and Witztum would run *one million* test experiments. The names and dates would be paired incorrectly 999,999 different ways. The correct list plus the incorrect lists would be searched for in the Book of Genesis. If the correct list ranked within the top thousand searches, Diaconis would sign a letter recommending publication.[80]

Rips and Witztum agreed. In the winter of 1991, computers at Hebrew University searched for one million sets of rabbis' names and dates as equidistant letter skips in the Book of Genesis. The computers searched non-stop.

And the results were astounding. The correct list of names and dates ranked 16/1,000,000 or p = 0.000016. Diaconis wrote a letter endorsing the research and the journal agreed to publish.

But the journal had one more requirement.

They wanted Rips and Witztum to calculate the confidence level for the experiment. The standard scientific confidence level is five percent, or one in twenty. What does that mean? The confidence level establishes that there is a less than one in twenty chance that the researcher got lucky. Less than one in twenty is considered a strong result and good enough for publication.

Risky experiments – when the outcome suggests something dangerous – need to demonstrate a higher level of confidence to get published. For example, the New England Journal of Medicine requires a confidence level of one in fifty (and sometimes one in one hundred) for issues considered life and death.

What was the confidence level Statistical Science required before they would publish a paper about equidistant letter skips in the Book of Genesis? One in twenty? One in fifty? One in one hundred?

How about one in one thousand.[81]

Do you think they were nervous?

One in one thousand is unheard of in the world of science. It is absurd. But the Journal of Statistical Science was not taking chances.

Rips and Witztum calculated the confidence level. The chance of the rabbi's names and dates of birth and death appearing in close proximity by accident – i.e. that the results were a fluke – were 1 in 62,500.

Yikes.

The paper was published in August 1994.[82]

The Institute of Mathematical Statistics publishes Statistical Science. They claimed the volume featuring equidistant letter skips was their most requested edition since the Institute was founded in 1935. The scientific community went nuts. It made headlines in the world of science. Publication set off a debate about the validity of the research. And it created a massive controversy.

Are you surprised?

The critics spent the next three years trying to debunk the codes. Among the critics were serious scientists and mathematicians. They combed the data with a fine-toothed comb. They paid a researcher to travel to Jewish cemeteries. The researcher examined the tombstones to confirm the correct spelling of the rabbis' names and the actual dates of birth and death. And they published a rebuttal in Statistical Science.[83]

The critics' attack was based on five mistakes found in the original experiment. Those mistakes were:

- ✵ Two of the rabbis' names were misspelled
- ✵ Two dates of death were incorrect
- ✵ An error in one of the formulas[84]

Rips and Witztum reran the experiment. They fixed the errors noted by the critics. And the critics were right. The confidence level of 1 in 62,500 based on the original experiment was incorrect. Once the data was corrected to account for the findings of the critics, the results came out differently.

Based on the information supplied by the critics, the new statistical confidence level came out to be 1 in 1,694,000.[85]

In other words, the critics improved the experiment. Why was the original confidence level so low? It was because the data was flawed. Once the data was corrected, the results were better.[86]

But the critics made a more serious claim as well. They claimed that Rips and Witztum manipulated their data. Specifically, the critics claimed that Rips and Witztum altered the spellings of the rabbis' names[87] in order to achieve desirable results. To prove their point, the critics ran an experiment – using a doctored list of names – and found similar results in *War and Peace*.

Did the critics have a point?

Not really.[88] Harold Gans, a Senior Cryptologic Mathematician for the U.S. Department of Defense, looked for the same list of rabbis used by Rips and Witztum. Instead of looking for the dates of death, he looked for the cities where the rabbis lived and died. His results were four times better than the original Rips/Witztum experiment: $4/1,000,000$ or $p = 0.000004$. And because Gans used the same list of names[89] as in the Rips/Witztum experiment, the success of his experiment implied that the Rips/Witztum experiment was legit.

Since the publication in Statistical Science, additional experiments were run.

One experiment searched for the names of the sixty-three volumes of the Talmud. The experiment had an advantage over the rabbi experiments: the name of each volume is fixed. And the names have been known since the completion of the Talmud in 500 CE. All the names were found. The names were encoded in close proximity. And the odds of the experiment being a fluke were 1 in 4,500,000.

The researchers looked for the names of the thirty-one cities conquered by Joshua. The cities are listed in the Book of Joshua. The spellings are fixed. The names were found and encoded in close proximity. The odds of it being a fluke were 1 in 50,000,000.

Some experiments failed. But most were successful and the results were astounding.

Search for Bible Codes online.

You will find codes in the New Testament. But these codes are not scientific. Most are silly.

You will find codes by charlatans claiming to predict the future. Good luck.

And you will find articles written by the codes critics.[90]

The codes critics' arguments attack the original article in Statistical Science. They do not discuss the experiment after it was rerun with the corrected data. They do not discuss the additional experiments using fixed spellings. They continue to bellyache about wiggle room in the first experiment.

In 2006, seven papers[91] were submitted to the 18th International Conference on Pattern Recognition[92] in Hong Kong. The papers were peer-reviewed.[93] The papers demonstrated that the methods and results from the original experiments were correct.

And the peer-reviewers agreed. The critics have remained silent. No one has challenged these papers.

Decide for yourself. Are equidistant letter skips in the Torah a fluke or were they encoded by design? If they were encoded by design, how did they get there?

Lock a group of monkeys in a room. Give each monkey a typewriter. If the monkeys type for long enough, they will eventually type the complete works of Shakespeare. But how many billions of years will it take?

At some point you have to say, "In theory it may be possible, but in reality it will never happen."

What about equidistant letter skips in the Torah? The odds are 1 in 1,694,000.[94] It is possible that they appeared in the Torah by accident. Do you think that is likely?

Take a look at a few more examples of equidistant letter skips in the Torah. These codes were not found as the result of scientific experiment *per se*, but they are interesting.

The Holocaust was a terrible war against the Jews. It happened in modern times. Are references to the Holocaust encoded in the Torah as equidistant letter skips?

Take a look (see Figure 10).

The computer found "the enemy" at an equidistant skip of nine. Not surprising. "Enemy" is a Hebrew word. You expect it to be there.

Below "enemy" is "Nazi" at an equidistant skip of twelve. Encoded is a phrase, "the Nazi enemy." Interesting.

Crossing the phrase, "the Nazi enemy," is "Germany" at a backwards skip of 155. "Berlin" is in close proximity to "Germany" and at a backwards skip of 4.

The phrase, "Jewish catastrophe," intersects "the Nazi enemy" as well. It is at an equidistant skip of 156.

Look at another example (see Figure 11). It starts with the same "Berlin" from the last example, but the view is set up differently.

Above "Berlin," and at a backwards skip of one, is "Nazi." Next to these words, and at a backwards skip of thirty-one, is "Hitler." Above "Hitler," and also at an equidistant skip of thirty-one, is *"rasha"* (Hebrew for "evil person"). And in case you didn't see the connection between Hitler and Berlin, "his city" appears at an equidistant skip of thirty-two.

If you read Hebrew, look closely at the Hebrew text. "Hitler" intersects the verse that says, "The heart of man is evil from his youth."

Look at one more example based on the same "Berlin" as before (see Figure 13).

Below "Berlin" is "Nazi" at a backwards skip of six. In close proximity to "Nazi" is "Amalek" at a large skip of 7,450. According to the Torah, Amalek was the nation sworn to destroy the Jewish people.

Intersecting "Amalek" at a skip of 3,725 is *slav keres*, the Hebrew word for swastika.

Look at a different cluster of words, unrelated to the last examples (see Figure 14).

The first two words are not exceptional. They are regular Hebrew words, similar to "the enemy" in the first Holocaust example. The first word is *"risha"* (the evil), a noun form of *rasha*. It is at a backwards

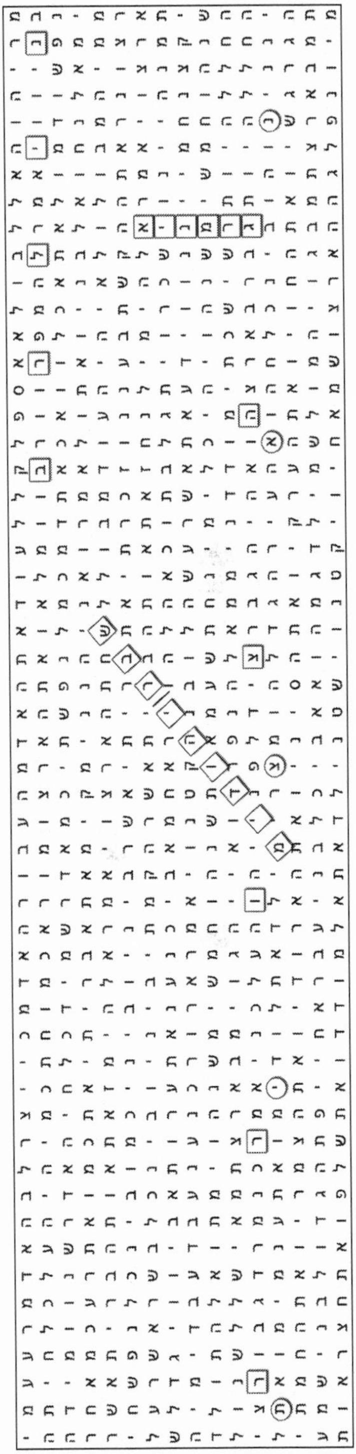

Figure 10.

Enemy	הצורר
Nazi	נאצית
Germany	גרמניא
Berlin	ברלין
Jewish Catastrophe	שבר יהודים

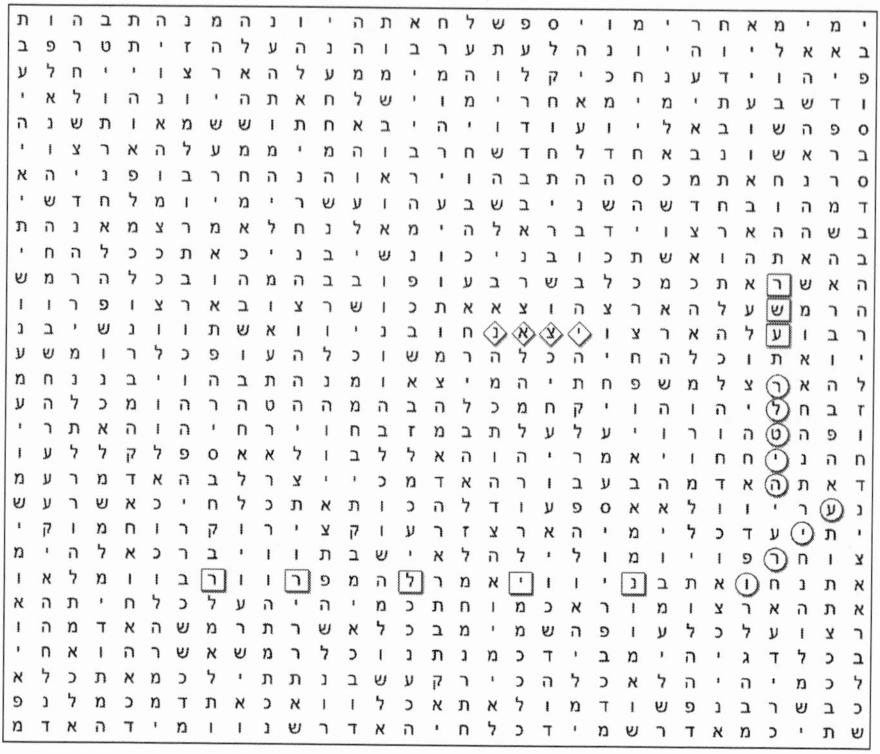

Figure 11.

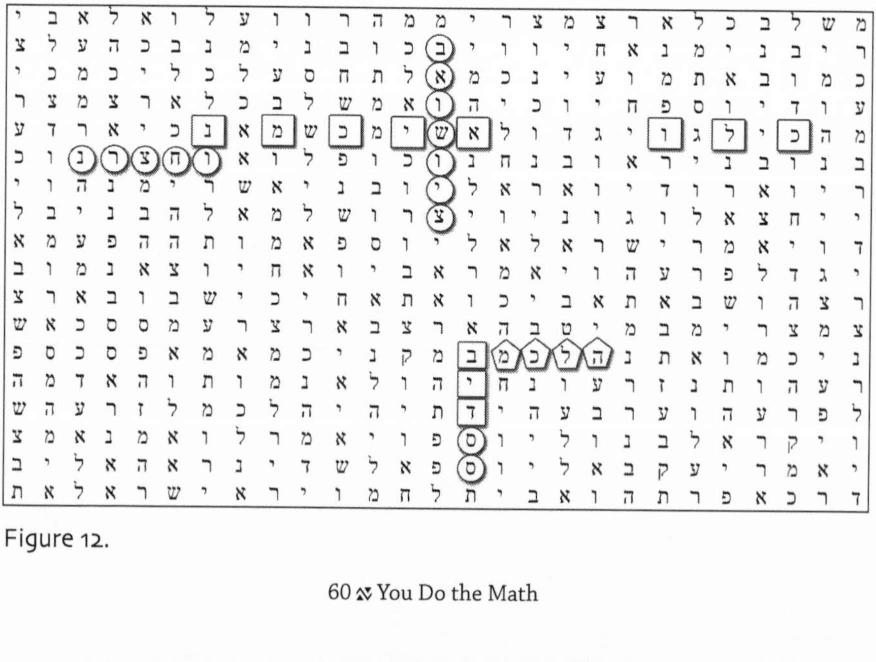

Figure 12.

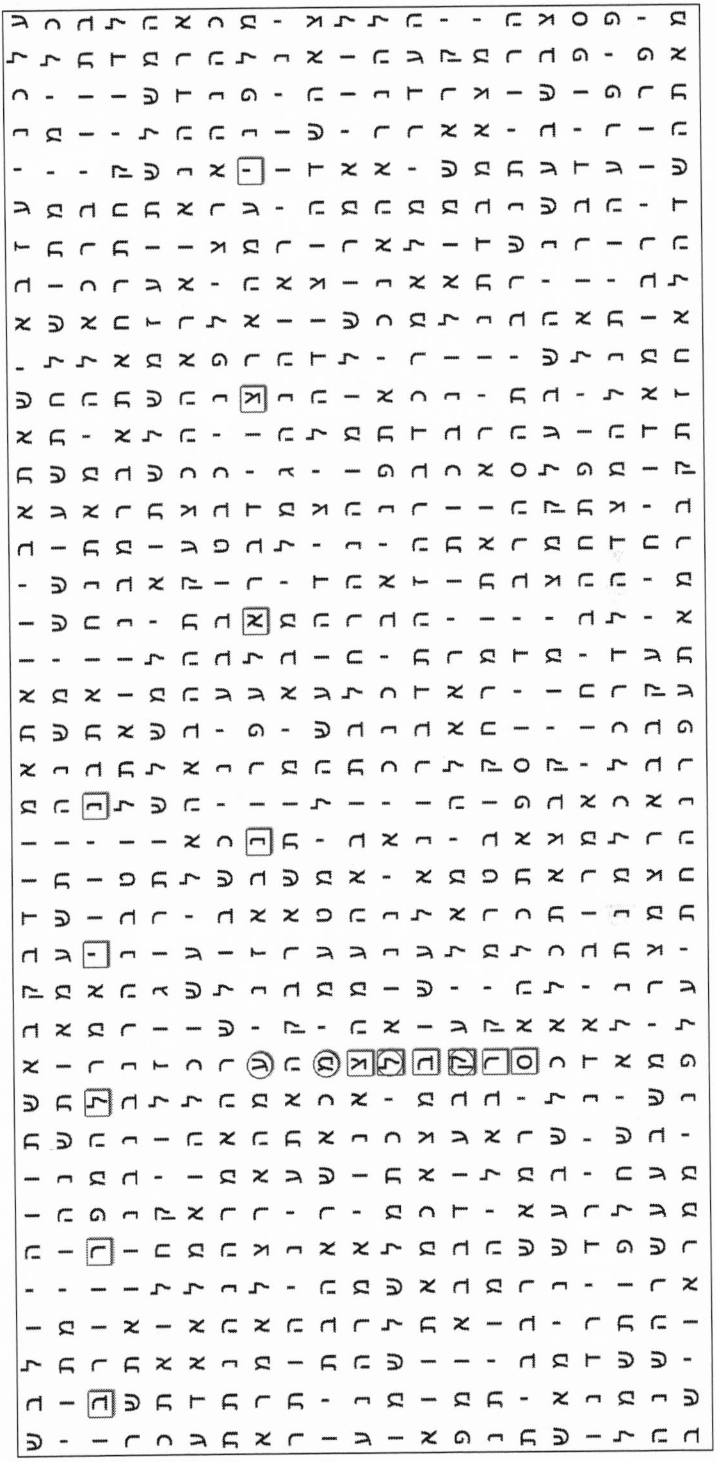

Figure 13.

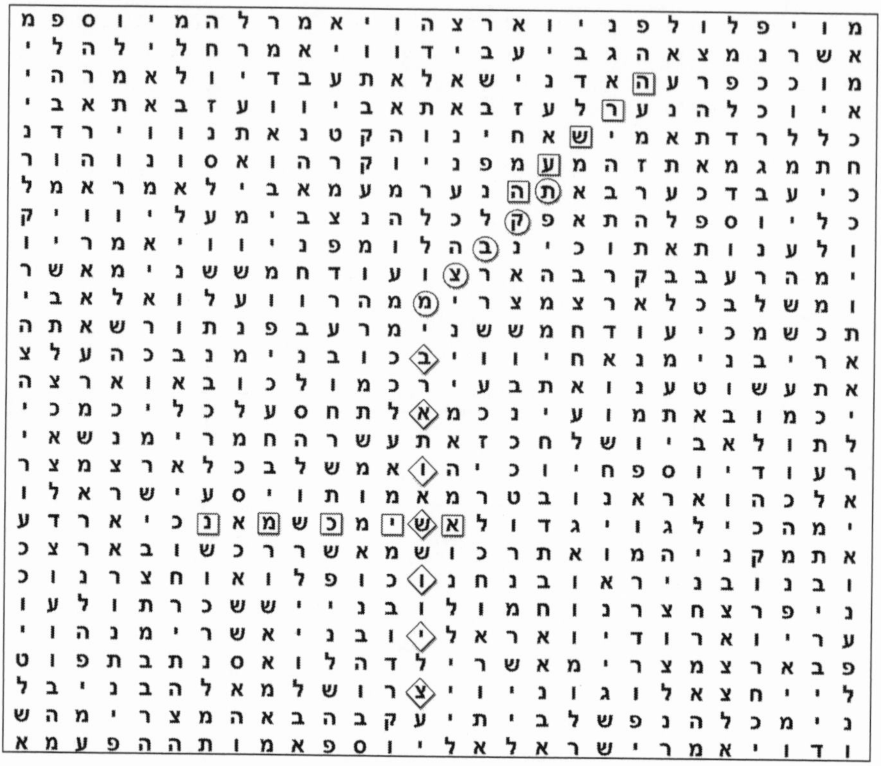

Figure 14.

Reference to Figure 11

Berlin	ברלין
Nazi	נאצי
Hitler	היטלר
evil	רשע
his city	עירו

Reference to Figure 12

in Auschwitz	באושוויץ
Eichmann	איכמן
Murdered	נרצחו
Destroyed	כלו
Destroyer	מכלה
by the SS	ביד סס

Reference to Figure 13

Berlin	ברלין
Nazi	נאצי
Amalek	עמלק
Swastika	צלב קרס

Reference to Figure 14

the evil	הרשע
will gather them	תקבצם
in Auschwitz	באושוויץ
Eichmann	איכמן

skip of 151. Next to it is the Hebrew word for "will gather them" also at a backwards skip of 151. The two codes form the phrase, "The evil will gather them."

Where will the Jews be gathered? Look at the next code.

Below the phrase, "The evil will gather them," and at an equidistant skip of 300, is the phrase, "In Auschwitz."

Intersecting "In Auschwitz," and at an equidistant skip of two, is "Eichmann." Eichmann was the chief architect of the Final Solution.

Look at a different view of "In Auschwitz" and "Eichmann" (see Figure 12).

Below "Eichmann" and at a backwards skip of one is "murdered." Eichmann murdered the Jews in Auschwitz. Also near this cluster is "*kilu*" (they were destroyed) at an equidistant skip of two.

Below "In Auschwitz" and at a backwards skip of one is "destroyer." What group carried out the destruction in Auschwitz? Next to "destroyer," and at an equidistant skip of 300 (similar to "In Auschwitz"), is the phrase, "By the S.S."

Look at one more example of equidistant letter skips about the Holocaust (see Figure 15).

"Eichmann" is an equidistant skip of two. The Nazis killed Jews in gas chambers. Gas was Eichmann's idea. "Gas" is an equidistant skip of two as well.

The gas the Nazi's used was Zyklon B. It was a cyanide-based pesticide. Between "Gas" and "Eichmann" is "Zyklon B" at a backwards skip of 9,180.

Incredible.

Can you use Torah codes to predict the future?

No.

Why not? It is impossible to predict the future using the Torah codes because you do not know how to read your results. You can interpret your findings, but your interpretation is just conjecture.

Pretend you searched for my name. Next to my name, you found "Messiah." Does that mean I am the messiah? Maybe. But it could mean that I am a friend of the messiah. Or it could mean that I am a false messiah. Or it could mean that I will teach a class about the messiah. Or it could mean that I will search the Torah for an equidistant letter skip of the word "messiah."

Do you get it? It could mean anything.

ו	ב	א	ת	א	כ	ל	ה	ה	ס	ו	ל	ל
ו	א	(ב)	י	ו	ו	ב	ש	י	ו	ר	ב	ד
ה	ב	ו	ה	כ	ר	ל	ש	כ	ל	נ	נ	ם
א	ם	ו	ב	א	ת	ש	א	י	ו	ש	ח	ק
ת	נ	ג	ל	י	ר	ח	א	כ	ע	ו	ז	ל
י	ש	א	א	ל	כ	י	ו	נ	ב	ל	א	ע
א	ו	ל	ו	א	נ	ה	ד	ר	א	ד	א	ם
ה	ה	ע	י	ל	ה	כ	י	ל	א	ו	א	ב
ב	ד	ל	ו	ב	ד	ת	נ	ש	ע	ל	ל	כ
ה	ת	ק	ר	ד	צ	ם	ב	י	ו	נ	ה	י
א	ם	(נ)	י	ם	ה	ו	ם	א	ו	ם	י	ה
[ז]	[ג]	ו	ב	א	ם	י	ו	ה	ר	א	ב	ת
ו	ב	א	ש	ל	ש	י	ב	ם	י	צ	ע	ל
ל	כ	י	ח	ל	ו	ר	ר	ק	ת	א	ו	נ
ו	ב	א	א	י	ל	א	ר	ם	א	י	ו	ם
ת	ם	ג	י	י	ל	א	ר	ם	א	ת	ו	י
ד	ל	ה	ו	כ	א	ם	ת	ם	י	נ	א	י
ב	ה	ל	ל	ם	ל	פ	ח	ו	ר	ח	צ	י
ע	ב	ו	ע	נ	ב	ק	ו	צ	ק	י	ה	ק
ב	א	ו	י	א	ש	י	ו	ר	י	ב	ב	ו
י	י	ד	א	ע	ם	ש	י	ר	ר	י	ו	א
ב	י	ע	ל	י	ת	י	י	ה	כ	י	ב	ק
א	ם	ד	ב	ה	ל	ד	נ	ה	ו	ר	ח	א
א	ל	ם	ב	ה	ל	א	נ	ת	ד	ר	ה	ל
ל	ג	ו	ע	ק	ע	י	א	ש	נ	ו	נ	ה
נ	ב	ל	י	ס	א	י	ו	ה	י	ל	ו	ה
ת	ו	ת	ב	ל	ם	ה	ד	ם	י	י	ד	ש
ש	א	ק	פ	ה	ר	ב	ב	ה	ע	ל	א	כ
א	פ	(ל)	ד	ה	ו	י	ה	ל	י	ה	ל	ח
ב	ל	ת	ז	ב	ח	כ	ת	ם	ת	ב	ה	ל
ו	כ	ג	ח	כ	ל	ה	צ	ע	ל	ו	נ	י
ה	ה	ו	א	י	ק	ח	ש	י	ו	ב	ו	ו
ו	ב	ק	ה	י	ל	א	ל	י	י	ל	ד	ו
י	ע	ש	ה	כ	ר	ד	ם	ן	ו	ה	א	ע
נ	י	ע	ע	ו	ר	ו	י	ח	ש	ב	כ	ם
ה	ת	ח	ו	ב	ק	ע	כ	ם	י	ל	א	ל
א	ב	י	ב	ם	ר	א	ם	ד	ת	ע	י	ו
ח	ר	(ק)	ת	ו	ל	א	ג	ל	ל	נ	נ	י
ה	ר	ש	ו	ע	ב	ש	ם	ב	ו	א	ו	ו
ל	ח	ו	פ	ה	י	ה	ב	ה	י	ב	פ	ד
א	א	ר	ע	ת	ו	כ	ש	ד	ו	י	י	י
ם	י	ש	י	ח	ש	ל	כ	ם	ש	ס	נ	ו
א	ב	י	ק	י	י	ת	ו	א	י	ו	ן	ו
ם	ל	ח	ד	י	ל	ח	ו	י	ת	ת	כ	ב
ו	ם	ה	א	פ	י	ת	ל	ו	פ	י	ו	ב
ת	ו	ב	ם	ה	ש	י	א	ב	ע	ם	ע	א
ו	ד	(י)	ת	א	י	י	ה	ם	א	א	ע	י
ס	ו	י	ס	ר	ל	ו	א	צ	ל	ת	י	י
ו	ק	ש	ת	א	י	ח	ה	ה	כ	ה	ם	א
ו	ו	ל	א	ו	ם	ל	א	י	א	ם	פ	י
ל	ד	ם	ת	ל	ש	ו	ש	ש	ר	ל	ל	נ
ח	ו	ל	ו	ה	י	י	ו	ב	ח	ב	א	ר
ו	ק	י	כ	א	ד	ב	כ	ל	ד	ב	ע	ו
ת	ם	א	ו	ם	נ	י	א	י	ע	ה	ר	ה
א	א	ל	[נ]	א	[ם]	ש	[כ]	ם	[י]	ש	[א]	ל
י	ה	(צ)	ם	ב	ו	ל	ד	ל	י	ר	ש	א
ה	ע	ר	ו	י	כ	פ	ל	ם	א	צ	י	ו

Eichmann	איכמן
Gas	גז
Zyklon B	ציקלון ב

Figure 15.

And in most cases, you don't know what to look for. Think about the terror attacks on 9/11. No one could have imagined them until they happened. How could someone search the Torah for a 9/11 code before 9/11? It is impossible.

But once it happened, it was easy to find. Look at these equidistant letter skips about 9/11, specifically the Twin Towers, (see Figure 16).

The Hebrew words for "Twin" and "Towers" appear as a backwards skip of one.

In 2001, the Hebrew date for September 11 was the 23rd of Elul. The Hebrew date intersects "Tower." It is a huge equidistant letter skip, but it works.

Below "Tower" is "Ishmael" at an equidistant skip of one. According to Jewish tradition (and Islamic tradition as well), the Arabs are descended from Ishmael. Also at a skip of one is "murdered." The descendents of Ishmael murdered about 3,000 people in the Twin Towers on September 11.

Look at one more example about 9/11 (see Figure 17).

"Airplane" is a backwards skip of thirty-nine. The phrase, "knocked down," is in close proximity and at a forward skip of thirty-nine. "Twin" is at an equidistant skip of seventy-one and "Towers" is nearby at a skip of thirty-six.

The researchers were bothered because "airplane" and "knocked down" are both in the singular – until they noticed "twice" in the text itself. The phrase "to die there" is also in the text.

Impressed?

Hundreds of significant equidistant letter skips were found: the 1991 Gulf War, Saddam Hussein's capture in 2003, his execution in 2006, the devastating tsunami of 2004, the Mumbai terrorist attacks in 2008, the death of Israeli astronaut Ilan Ramon in 2003, the horrible murder of Rabbi Abuchatzirah in 2011, and the list goes on.

If something big happens, someone finds a code for it. And many of these codes share common features: they appear as clusters of words, usually in close proximity, and often at their minimal skip.

You can't make this stuff up.

Think about it.

You can't say the Jews hid equidistant letter sequences about the future when they were wandering in the desert. That would be impos-

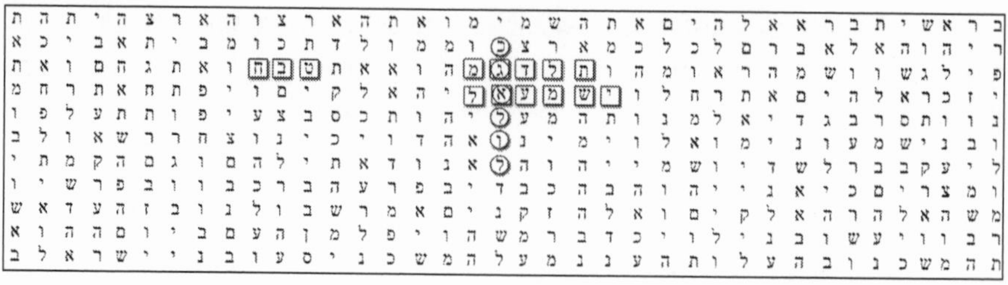

Figure 16.

Reference to Figure 16

Twin	התאומים
Towers	מגדלת
23rd Elul (Sept 11)	כג אלול
Ishmael	ישמעאל
Murdered	טבח

Reference to Figure 17

Air plane	מטוס
Knocked down	הפיל
Twin	התאומים
Towers	מגדלי
Twice	פעמים
To die there	למות שם

Figure 17.

sible. You can't say this phenomenon exists in every large book. Rips and Witztum ran one million test experiments; the phenomenon is exclusive to the Torah.

So what do you think?

Consider the evidence.

Who do you think wrote the Torah?

Identifying Information:
The Pig's Foot

Information Only the Author Knows

How does an ATM work?

You insert your card and enter your PIN. The machine gives you money. It won't give you money if the PIN is wrong. PIN stands for Personal Identification Number. You know it. Nobody else does.

Online security is similar. You need a password to check your email, to pay your bills, or to join a social networking site. In addition, most online services ask specific security questions like, "What is your mother's maiden name?" "What was the name of your first pet?" "What was the name of your high school mascot?" "What was the make of your first car?" You know this information. Nobody else does.

Does the Torah have a PIN?

Look at the kosher laws. The kosher laws contain information that only the author could know. Assuming the author was God.

The kosher laws are complex. They apply to everything you eat including meat, plants, fruits, vegetables, bugs, and processed foods.

Take meat for example. How do the kosher laws apply to meat?

Most meat is not kosher. That is because most animals are not kosher. A kosher animal has two distinguishing characteristics: it has split hooves and it chews its cud. It is rare that an animal has both features.

What are split hooves?

Look at the animal's foot. Does it have a paw or a hoof? If it has a paw, it is not kosher. If it has a hoof, is the hoof a big block – like a horse? Or is it split in two – like a cow (it looks like two big, hard toes)?

If it is split, that is one distinguishing characteristic.

The other is cud chewing.

A kosher animal has multiple stomachs. It eats grass or grain, chews it, swallows it, brings it back to its mouth to chew again, and then swallows into a different stomach. An animal that does this is a ruminant. (The process is called rumination.)

Kosher animals have split hooves and chew their cud. They must have both features. One isn't enough.

But if the animal has both, it is kosher. No more information is necessary. Split hooves and rumination are the only things to look for. Nothing else.

Are cows kosher? Yes, they have split hooves and chew their cud.

Are lions kosher? No, they don't have split hooves or chew their cud.

Elephants, bears, snakes, monkeys, and mice are not kosher – they don't have split hooves or chew their cud. Cows, deer, goats, and sheep are kosher – they have split hooves and chew their cud.

How about camels? No. They chew their cud but they don't have split hooves. How about pigs? No. The have spilt hooves but don't chew their cud.

Simple.

Look at an animal. Look at its feet. Look at the goo in its mouth. If the foot is split and the mouth is pasty, *bon appétit*.

The Torah mentioned these two signs. And that is all it needed to say. It taught a simple rule to determine if an animal is kosher or not.

And that is what makes these verses in the Book of Leviticus so unusual:

> Among the cud-chewing, hoofed animals, these are the ones you may not eat: The camel shall be unclean to you although it brings up its cud, since it does not have a split hoof. The *shafan* shall be unclean to you although it brings up its cud, since it

does not have a split hoof. The *arneves* shall be unclean to you although it brings up its cud, since it does not have a split hoof. The pig shall be unclean to you although it has a split hoof, since it does not chew its cud. Do not eat the flesh of these animals.[95]

Why does the Torah list these four animals? True, they are exceptions to the rule – each animal has one sign but not the other. But listing exceptions is unnecessary. The rule is already clear: both signs, kosher; one sign or no signs, not kosher. Simple.

And if you look carefully at the Hebrew grammar, it makes it clear that these four animals are the *only* exceptions.[96] The camel, *shafan*, and *arneves* are the only animals that ruminate but don't have split hooves. The pig is the only animal that has split hooves but doesn't ruminate.

That is a gutsy thing to say.

What happens if you discover another animal with only one sign? Oops.

Why take the risk? Listing the exceptions is risky and unnecessary. The kosher laws are clear without the extra information.

Think about it. People discover new animals all the time. People discovered new animals in the ancient world, too.

The ancient Egyptians had zoos. They had animals from all over Africa. They even had bears.[97] The Jews were slaves in Egypt 3,300 years ago. It isn't farfetched to think that some Jewish slaves visited the zoos of their masters.

Or imagine a different scenario. Maybe a rich Egyptian master took his Jewish slave with him on vacation. If he vacationed up the Nile in Sudan or Ethiopia – and wandered into the wilderness – the master and his slave saw new creatures they never saw before. Exotic beasts live in distant lands.

These are possibilities. You can probably think of a few more.

And if an ex-slave helped write the Torah, he would not state: "Four animals have one kosher sign, but not both. There are no other exceptions." He knows that someone could discover another animal.

Why gamble?

But is it a gamble if you know that you're right?

The Torah was written 3,300 years ago. Thousands of new animals have been discovered. And none of the new animals are a fifth exception. Pigs are still the only non-ruminating animals with split hooves. Camels, *shafans*, and *arneveses*, are still the only ruminating animals without split hooves.

Look at this quote from the Talmud:

> Was Moses a hunter or an archer? This is to answer those who say that the Torah isn't from heaven.[98]

Moses was not familiar with every type of animal in the world. But God was. It was risky for Moses to list only four possible exceptions. It wasn't risky for God.

But you probably have a question.

What is a *shafan* and what is an *arneves*? Camel and pig are familiar. *Shafan* and *arneves* are not.

The *shafan* and *arneves* are most likely both extinct species.[99]

How convenient.

If someone discovers an animal that ruminates but doesn't have split hooves, just claim it is a *shafan* or *arneves*. The author inserted a fudge factor into the text. He covered all his bases.

But what about the pig?

The pig is the only animal listed that has split hooves but doesn't ruminate. The Torah doesn't include an extinct animal to cover in case a new animal with split hooves that doesn't ruminate is discovered.

And scientists have classified thousands of animals since the Torah was written. Pigs are still the only animals that have spilt hooves but don't chew their cud.

Incredible.

Moses wasn't a zoologist. He didn't know the Torah's PIN number. But the author did.

Who do you think he was?

Transmission: A Funny Thing Happened on the Way From Mount Sinai

The Jewish Experience at Mount Sinai

Once there was a king.

He was a great king. His subjects loved him. He was kind. He was just. He won wars.

But he wasn't going to live forever. He worried about his replacement. "Who will be the next king?"

It bothered him. He wanted the next generation to be strong. He wanted his legacy to continue. But he didn't know what to do. He had three sons – each son was a potential ruler – but he wasn't sure who to chose.

His oldest son was a stable and good man. He had great character. People respected him. He would make a good king.

But he wasn't the only choice. There was his second son. His second son was the Minister of Finance. He was a financial genius. Every time he spoke the markets went up. He was great with money and great for the economy. But he was boring. The masses didn't relate to him.

And there was his youngest son. His youngest son was a great warrior. The people loved him. He was charismatic. He was good looking. His wife was a celebrity. He was a dynamic speaker. But he wasn't as smart as his older brothers. He might not be able to handle the job.

Which son to choose? The king was worried. He ran through different scenarios in his head. He discussed options with his advisors and friends. It wasn't an easy decision. He didn't want to make a mistake.

One day, while he was thinking about which son to choose, he died.

Oops.

His death was sudden and unexpected. The nation was heartbroken. A thirty-day period of mourning was declared. And the coronation of the new king was set for the week after the funeral.

But no one knew who would be the new king. Each son wanted the job. Each son knew his father considered him a possibility. But the king died too soon.

People took sides. In the court, ministers and officials lobbied for their man. On the streets people held signs and staged rallies. The newspapers wrote editorials. The tabloids went nuts. The princesses stopped talking to each other. Stores closed. The army called up the reserves. The situation was tense. The nation was on edge. Would there be a Civil War? Something had to give.

One morning one of the sons called a meeting in the palace. He was very excited. He wanted to speak only to his brothers. He kicked out the servants and bolted the doors.

"What's going on?" The other brothers asked.

"You won't believe me." He said.

"We'll believe you." They said.

"Last night dad came to me in a dream. Guess what he told me."

The brothers didn't know what to say.

"Dad told me that I am the next king. Isn't that great? Long live the King."

Is it true? Maybe. Do you believe him?

Consider the situation.

Did he have a dream? Probably. Did his father speak from the grave? He says he did.

But how do you know? He can't prove it. You may believe him if you trust him.

Do his brothers trust him? I doubt it. They want to be the new king, too. Plus, they have a good claim, "If dad really has the power to speak from the grave, wouldn't he tell all three of us?"

Think about it. If the king came to all three brothers, on the same night, in the same dream, and he told each person the same thing – so-and-so is the new king – they would believe it. They have to believe it. They don't need proof. They saw it themselves.

Imagine the three of them the next morning. They compare notes. Spooky? Yes. But it happened and they know it.

Do you believe things people tell you? Of course you do. Would you believe a story about a drunken brawl? Probably. If the story is just a story – and it isn't about you – you accept it as is. Would you ask for proof? Probably not. You don't need proof. But if the story is about you – i.e. that you were in a drunken brawl – you want evidence.

In most cases – whether the story is mundane, news, local gossip, politics, a dream, weird, or supernatural – if it is about you or impacts your life you want proof. If it isn't, you don't.

Religion, bibles, prophecy, dreams, and communication with the dead are supernatural phenomena. So are claims by psychics, sooth-sayers, tarot cards, Ouija boards, crystal balls, voodoo, ghosts, and UFOs. Some people believe that supernatural, metaphysical, other-worldly experiences happen all the time. Many people don't. And it usually doesn't matter. You don't care if your neighbor says he saw Elvis, Martians, or the Virgin Mary. He can believe what he wants. It doesn't affect you.

But what if it affects you?

If it affects you, you demand evidence. If Elvis told your neighbor to build a large plastic shrine in his backyard and hundreds of people stand on your porch every day to see it, you want proof.

And you want solid proof.

Your neighbor needs to get you a meeting with Elvis. A meeting with Elvis will convince you that the shrine is important. But if he can't arrange a meeting with Elvis – he tells you to take his word for it – you will make him take down the shrine. His claim lacks credibility.

Take this a step further. Pretend you are God. How would you convince a group of people to follow your laws? Would you pick a person, make him your prophet, and tell him your message? Maybe. But isn't that as weak as a message from Elvis?

If you are God – and you are bigger than Elvis – you can do anything. Why limit your message to a single witness? Tell the entire group. Give them an experience they will never forget. Stamp it on their collective subconscious. Make it a part of their history. Make it a holiday. Make them celebrate the anniversary with cheesecake and barbeques.

History works this way. You experience something – war, natural disaster, a terrorist attack, a rock concert – anything. You tell your children. They believe you. And your credibility increases with the size of the event. A bigger event is more important and easier to believe than a smaller one.

Think about it. World War II was more important than an attempted coup in South America. It was too big. It affected too many people. Too many economic, political, geopolitical, religious, philosophical, and moral issues were affected by it. You know it happened.

How about a coup in South America? Did it happen? Maybe. But you need to look it up. It wasn't big enough to affect you. Your father didn't tell you about it.

You don't believe your neighbor's claim that Elvis told him to build a shrine in his backyard. It is a silly claim. He doesn't have proof. (And you are bothered because it affects you.)

But you would believe him if he told you that 75,000 people attended Elvis's funeral in Memphis. The event was too big.

Think about history. You accept the claims of previous generations. You accept them as fact. Stories about empires, great leaders, wars, and natural disasters you accept at face value. You don't question claims made by nations or large groups of people. Too many people were involved. Too many people with different opinions, backgrounds, interests, beliefs, points of view, and biases claim the same thing. Too much subsequent history is based on it. And you don't need hard evidence like documents, ruins, artifacts, or pictures to prove it. The strength of the claim is enough.

Do you accept everything you hear? No. Claims made by small groups or individual witnesses are harder to prove. You won't be concerned if the claim doesn't affect you. But if it does, you need proof.

If your neighbor saw Elvis, or your brother became king in a dream, you want evidence before you accept it.

Single-witness claims make the history books. But do you believe the claim? Sometimes you do. Look at this example. Do you believe it?

Two thousand years ago, the Romans conquered Egypt. That is a fact. It's a fact that Julius Caesar went to Egypt too. And it's a fact that Rome was in the midst of a civil war when he went there.

These are historical facts. Thousands of people were involved; soldiers, merchants, peasants, refugees, world leaders, and old world despots. Caesar's visit set in motion a chain of events that destroyed the Roman Republic. The Roman occupation directly impacted the Roman economy. And Rome stayed in Egypt for hundreds of years. You can't make that stuff up.[100]

So far so good.

Rome in the waning days of the Republic was in turmoil. It was a nation racked by civil war, unrest, and political instability. Julius Caesar was on the ascent and battling Pompey the Great – his son-in-law, former partner in government, and a brilliant general – for ultimate power.

Pompey made his way across the Mediterranean to Alexandria, Egypt. Ptolemy XIII – a boy Pharaoh who was battling Cleopatra, his older sister, for control of Egypt – came out to greet him. Ptolemy tricked Pompey into coming ashore, murdered him, cut off his head, and pickled it like a tomato.

Caesar arrived in Alexandria a few months later. Ptolemy wanted Caesar to help him destroy Cleopatra. He sent him Pompey's pickled head as a gift. He thought Caesar would be thrilled.

He was wrong. Caesar wept.

Caesar made his way into the city, took over the port and the royal palace, and demanded exorbitant taxes from the locals. He offered to referee the dispute between Ptolemy and his sister. But he wasn't getting involved.

Or so he thought.

Cleopatra was not going to lose Egypt to her brother and Caesar was going to help her. How? She had a plan.

An Egyptian servant carried a rug into Caesar's headquarters. Caesar was curious. "Why are you bringing me a rug?" He unrolled the rug. Cleopatra jumped out.

"Hello big fellow, slaughter any Gauls lately?"

Caesar was smitten. And the rest is history.

Cleopatra was soon pregnant with Caesar's child. Ptolemy went into a rage and unleashed the mob and his soldiers against Caesar. Anarchy. And then Ptolemy drowned in the Nile. The mob calmed down. The soldiers went home. And Caesar installed Cleopatra as the undisputed ruler of Egypt. To seal the deal she married her ten-year old brother.[101]

Did it happen? Most of it did. The civil war, the murder of Pompey, and Caesar's visit to Egypt are well-documented events that were witnessed by a lot of people. Moreover, the implications of these events were far reaching and long-lasting. It is known that Cleopatra was pregnant, too; she claimed Caesar was the father and their son ultimately became a Pharaoh as well.

But was Cleopatra really smuggled into the palace in a rug?

Caesar said she was. Do you believe him? He was the only witness. If you believe him, it happened. If you don't, it didn't. His word is the only evidence.

Imagine Caesar at the officers club the next morning with the guys. "You aren't going to believe what happened last night. It was wild. The princess was smuggled into my room. She was rolled up in a rug."

The event managed to make the history books even though Caesar was the only witness. Do you care? Probably not. It is a fun story. There is no reason to doubt it. And the implications of believing it are minimal. It doesn't matter if they met when Cleopatra was rolled out of a rug, at a ball, or at a boring diplomatic meeting surrounded by ambassadors and attaché cases. The important thing is that they met, not *how* they met. You can believe Caesar, but you don't have to. And it doesn't matter if you do.

That is why a single-witness claim is a weak historical claim. You accept it if it doesn't matter. But if it matters, you need more evidence.

How about a small group? A small group is easier to believe than a single witness. More people claim the same thing. More people verify the same facts. More people tell overlapping stories. It is harder to make up a story when a group of people has to agree on the details.

A small group has credibility.

But a small group claim isn't foolproof. A charismatic leader can manipulate a small group of people. He can use social pressure and group dynamics to prod, coerce, force, or take over the group.

In 1978, 908 people committed suicide in Jonestown, Guyana. They were members of the People's Temple. Their leader was Jim Jones.

Jones gained national prominence as the leader of the People's Temple. Among his friends and close political connections were people like Vice President Walter Mondale, Rosalynn Carter, and San Francisco politician Harvey Milk. He started the People's Temple in Indiana but made his name after moving to San Francisco. The Temple practiced "Apostolic Socialism."

In 1974 the People's Temple moved to Guyana (on the northern coast of South America) and established Jonestown, a utopian socialist agricultural paradise. By 1978, almost a thousand people lived in Jonestown.

But Jonestown wasn't perfect. A few people defected and left Jonestown. Tim and Grace Stoen were members of the People's Temple. They defected and left Jonestown. But the Stoens were unable to take their son John with them. Jones claimed he was John's father. The Stoens went to court, fought for custody, and won. But Jones wouldn't let John leave. The Guyanese government was unwilling to intervene. The Stoens appealed to the U.S. State Department and wrote to members of Congress. Jones and members of the People's Temple did so as well.

In November 1978 Leo Ryan, a Congressman from Northern California, went to Guyana on a fact-finding mission. He knew the father of someone involved with the People's Temple. Reporters, cameramen, and officials from his Congressional office went with him.

Ryan's group spent a day in Jonestown. They interviewed Jones and Temple members, spent the night, and spoke with a few people who wanted to get out. The next day, as they were leaving, Temple loyalists killed Ryan and four others.

Jones was paranoid. Ryan's visit fueled his paranoia. He preached after Ryan was murdered. "This is what I warned you about. They are coming to get us. They want to ruin our utopia, steal our children, and destroy our way of life. Our only chance for salvation is Revolutionary Suicide."

Jones preached about conspiracies and fascists. He preached about suicide. He preached about dying with dignity. Ryan's visit was proof he was right. And Ryan's murder silenced any dissent.

The Jonestown community followed Jones's orders. They filled a punch bowl with Flavor-Aid and laced it with cyanide. Most people drank from the communal bowl and died. Some women gave Flavor-Aid to their children. Whole families killed themselves. Jones shot himself in the head. A few people fled. An elderly man slept through it. A deaf man didn't hear the announcement calling everyone together.

More than 900 people committed suicide. When it was over, it was the largest mass killing of Americans until 9/11.[102]

The story of the People's Temple illustrates the weakness of a small group. A charismatic leader can convince a group – even a large group of 900 people – of anything. The claim of a small group still trumps a single-witness, but a small group has weaknesses that if exploited damage the claim's believability.

Think about history again. Some historical claims – like those by a small group or a single witness – are weak. Others aren't.

What is a strong historical claim?

An event experienced by a large group or nation. These claims are accepted as fact. You don't consider the French Revolution, the Protestant Reformation, the Battle of Hastings, the Spanish Inquisition, Alexander the Great, Ivan the Terrible, the fall of the Roman Empire, or Attila the Hun to be myths, fairytales, or massive capitalist conspiracies. The events happened. The people existed.

How do you know?

They were too big. Too many witnesses. Too many people were involved. Too many people with different interests, opinions, values, beliefs, and points of view were affected. Too many different people told the same story. Too much subsequent history is dependent on these events.

Is every detail accurate or correct? Of course not. But the events happened.

You know they did.

And you don't need to visit ruins, gravesites, or museums to know it. A national claim speaks for itself.

Look at the Vietnam War. Did it happen? Of course it did. It changed America. And it doesn't matter that it happened far away or that most Americans never went there. Most Americans knew someone who went. Many knew someone who died. Many were concerned about the draft, politics, morality, and necessity of the war. It affected the economy, elections, books, music, movies, television, the way news was reported, and subsequent culture and history. It changed the way people thought. It changed the way people related to government. It changed college campuses. It was the first TV war. And it was the defining event of a generation.

Do you think the Vietnam War was a lie? Was it a left-wing conspiracy to foment civil unrest, forward a leftist agenda, and increase the power of the media? Unlikely. Do you need documents, photos, or a trip to Vietnam to prove that it happened? No.

Vietnam was an event that America experienced. You know it happened.

Is every story true? Not necessarily. In the 2008 presidential election John McCain made a big deal out of his years at the Hanoi Hotel. Was he there? Is his story accurate? You have no reason to doubt him. He probably isn't lying. But how do you know? And even if he is lying, so what? You still know that the Vietnam War happened. John McCain's memory doesn't affect that.

Go back 2,000 years. The Punic Wars – the three great wars between Carthage and Rome – did they happen? There isn't much archeological evidence. Original documents don't exist. Most accounts of the wars were written after the fact. How do you know they happened?

Rome fought three wars with Carthage from 264-146 BCE. At the start of the first war, Carthage dominated the Mediterranean. Rome was an up-and-coming city in central Italy. They fought over territory, trade, and for dominance of the Mediterranean. The wars led to the rise of the Roman navy, an invasion of Northern Italy, military innovations, a near siege of Rome, the destruction of Carthage, and an ultimate Roman victory. Rome's victory established it as the dominant power in the Mediterranean and set the stage for Rome's conquest of most of the ancient world.[103]

Are the Punic Wars myth or fact?

They are fact. You know they happened. And you know the same way you know about Vietnam. The Punic Wars were an event central to the development of Rome. Every Roman citizen was affected.

They changed the Roman economy. They changed the Roman military. They changed Roman politics. And they were the impetus for 500 years of subsequent Roman history. You don't need documents, archeology, or written accounts to know the Punic Wars really happened.

You know they happened because Rome said they happened.

And that is enough. When a nation claims an event as its history, the claim is enough. It is a fact.

You can manipulate a small group. A single witness can lie. But a nation cannot lie. A nation is too big.

Is every claim about the Punic Wars true? Did Cato the Elder really end every speech, "Carthage must be destroyed?" Maybe. But like John McCain and the Hanoi Hotel, it doesn't matter. Every detail may not be true, but the Punic Wars are history. That is indisputable.

Think about recent history.

Tell an American 9/11 didn't happen. It's preposterous. There were millions of eyewitnesses. The evidence was overwhelming. And every American knows it's his history.

Millions of New Yorkers saw the Twin Towers crumble. If you weren't in New York, you know where you were when you heard the news. The country stopped. The stock market crashed. Businesses shut down. Manhattan was closed to incoming and outgoing traffic. The phones stopped working. President Bush grounded flights, closed airports, spoke to the nation that night, and called a joint session of Congress soon after. A new government agency – the Department of Homeland Security – was created. 9/11 was the justification for the wars in Afghanistan and Iraq. It was the only news story for weeks after the attack. It dominated the 2004 presidential election.

And everyone was affected. Daily life changed. Armed soldiers were in malls, train stations, airports, and other public places. You needed a passport to take a train from New York to Boston. Photo ID was required to enter tall buildings. Airport security was a mess. And many of these changes are still in effect years later.

9/11 was an event like the Kennedy Assassination or the Japanese attack on Pearl Harbor. It was a transformative moment in national history. Millions of people experienced it, remember it, and were changed by it.

Was it a hoax?

How do you fool so many people? How do you change the New York skyline? How do explain the millions of eyewitnesses? How do you explain the subsequent history that was based on it?

You can't. 9/11 is history. Future generations will know about it and accept it as fact.

How will they know? The material evidence is gone. The planes were destroyed on impact. The remains of the buildings were removed within a year of the attack. New buildings will stand on the site of the old.

And the witnesses won't live forever. Within a hundred years of the attack most of the witnesses, survivors, and their families will be dead.

How will future generations know?

It won't be from movies, news footage, old magazines, newspapers, Wikipedia, or a high school history class.

Future generations will know because nations don't lie. They can't.

In the years after 9/11 millions of people will tell their children what they saw, how they felt, where they were, how they were affected, and how they were inconvenienced. If they were in New York that day – or knew someone who was – they will talk about that too. They'll talk at the event's anniversary, family gatherings, significant events, or whenever. People talk, reflect, and reminisce all the time. Everyone does. You do it too. You talk about history, where you were, how you felt, and how you were affected.

That's how I know about the Kennedy assassination. My mother's older sister got married that weekend. My grandparents decided not to postpone the wedding, but the assassination was all anyone talked about. My father was still in college at the time. He went to the funeral in Washington. He sat on a lamppost and took pictures.

I heard these stories from my parents. I told them to my children. The details are particular to my family, but the assassination isn't. My family's memories are in the context of history. The stories were confirmed by other stories I heard from people my parents' age, friends, teachers, and others. The photos, films, and things I read added details and color. But they weren't telling me anything I didn't already know.

History is a nation remembering, sharing, confirming, and preserving its collective experiences. The events are interrelated, complex, part of a string of other events, and the basis for what comes next. You can't make it up.

Is every detail correct? No. But something happened. There are differences of opinion, different ways of looking at an event, details that mean more to different people, and aspects that are emphasized or exploited for political, social, or other reasons. There are stories that are false as well. But that doesn't change the fact that something happened.

You know that Kennedy was assassinated. You know that two planes flew into the Twin Towers on 9/11.

Think about one more thing.

How will your grandchildren know that the Holocaust happened? In fifty years most of the witnesses – survivors, refugees, liberating soldiers, and journalists – will be dead. Why will your grandchildren believe you? Do you have hard evidence?

You can show them photographs. But how do you know the photos weren't doctored in a lab? Computer technology is good enough to alter, enhance, change, and even create images. You can do that now. Imagine how much better the technology will be in fifty years.

How about videos and interviews with survivors? Interviews are easy to fake as well. How do you know the "survivors" weren't actors? It isn't hard or expensive to hire people to play the role of survivor.

Could you prove it with films, newsreels, reports, and archived materials taken by the soldiers liberating the camps? Same problem. These could also be manipulated, special effects, or fakes. It isn't hard to do.

You could bring your grandchildren to Poland to tour the camps.

Unfortunately, even the camps don't prove anything. There are many memorials built on the sites of the camps, but not much evidence of mass murder.

I toured the camps a few summers ago. I was surprised by the lack of evidence of Nazi atrocities. Treblinka was a memorial in the woods – trees and monuments – but no buildings, graves, barracks, or evidence of mass murder. At Majdanek, our tour guide apologized because the restoration of the gas chambers wasn't done correctly. The doors were put in the wrong walls and the chamber itself was in the wrong part of the building. It wasn't an accurate representation of what was originally there. Auschwitz was originally military barracks. The Hapsburgs built it in the 1800's at the time of the Austro-Hungarian Empire. And it looks like military barracks. A future archeologist digging in the country-formerly-known-as-Poland would not consider Auschwitz as anything other than an army base. I doubt he would consider it a death camp based on his findings.

The number of people killed is difficult to believe as well. Would you believe a story about the mass murder of 6,000,000 people? It is a big number to swallow.

Holocaust deniers say these things. They claim the photographs, interviews, news reports, and camps are fakes or exaggerations. Although they admit something happened, they twist the evidence to tell a different story. For example, they agree the Nazis were horrible people. They agree that many people were killed. But they say that those killed were political prisoners. And the real number of people killed was more like 100,000. Were Jews killed? Yes. But so were a lot of other people. The Nazis targeted communists. Everyone knows many Jews were communists. The popular story of the Holocaust as the mass extermination of Jews was a Zionist plot to arouse world sympathy and justify the creation of the State of Israel.

Does that make you angry?

Why? How do you know the Holocaust really happened? How do you know Holocaust deniers are lying?

You know the Holocaust happened because it is your history. You know it happened just like you know Vietnam, 9/11, and the Kennedy Assassination happened. And your grandchildren will know it too.

The Holocaust was a transformative Jewish national experience. Every Jew was affected. Hundreds of survivors, eyewitnesses, concerned relatives, families, journalists, and returning soldiers talked about what they saw, witnessed, and experienced. They talked about how they felt. They shared the stories with their children and grandchildren. They spoke in public, wrote books, memoirs, and published their diaries.

The Holocaust convinced many Jews of the need for Israeli independence. It was the motivation for violence against the British in Mandatory Palestine. It was the reason for a massive controversy in Israel over accepting money from West Germany. It was the guilt trip many parents laid on their children as a reason against intermarriage. It led to the creation of museums, charities, hospitals, and the rebuilding of Hasidic dynasties.

And the world changed. The Holocaust was a reason for the establishment of the United Nations, the International Court of Justice, and War Crimes trials.

Everyone has stories in their families about survivors or meeting survivors. My mother told me about the survivors she saw in Brooklyn when she was a girl. They were tough people and had numbers tattooed on their arms. They made a strong impression on her. Every family has stories like these.

You can't make up a nation's history. Too many people tell the same story – different names, places, opinions, and circumstances – but still the same basic story. Too many details are interrelated, corroborated, and confirmed through multiple tellings by different people in independent settings.

The Holocaust is your history. You know it happened. It is impossible to fake. The evidence is too overwhelming, too intermingled, and too substantiated to be a hoax.

Did every story happen? Is every detail accurate? Probably not. But did something happen? Certainly.

What about ancient Jewish history?

The Jewish people lived in Egypt 3,300 years ago. They were slaves. They wanted freedom. They wanted to leave Egypt. Moses – a fugitive exiled hundreds of miles from Egypt - returned to save them. He was successful.

The Jews left Egypt. They survived oppression, genocide, and witnessed open miracles as they escaped. The first place they stopped was the foot of Mount Sinai. They set up camp.[104]

The Jews took a census when camped at Mount Sinai. They counted men over the age of twenty: there were 603,550. Assume most of these men were married: that makes 1.2 million adults. Assume most of these couples had children. A good guess is that between two and three million Jews were encamped at the foot of Mount Sinai. That isn't a small group. It is a nation.

Moses climbed Mount Sinai. God spoke to him when he got to the top.

God said, "I am going to speak to you in front of the nation. They will hear My voice. They will believe in you forever."

Not bad. If Elvis told your neighbor, "I will explain the reason for the plastic shrine. Gather your neighbors and let them hear my voice." You would be impressed.

But the Jews wanted better. They told Moses, "We didn't schlep to the middle-of-nowhere to hear God talk to you. We want God to talk to us."[105]

God agreed. He told Moses, "Tell the people to prepare. Build a barrier around the mountain. No intimacy for three days, bathe, and put on clean clothes."

Moses returned to the people. They prepared. Three days later the mountain looked like a volcano.

But that was not all. The people saw fire, smoke, thunder, and lightening. They heard a ram's horn get louder and louder. They saw sounds and heard colors.

And then God spoke. He didn't speak to His prophet – Moses – in private. He didn't appear to one person in a dream. He spoke to the nation, live and in person.

Imagine if the king returned from the grave. He called together his sons. He also invited his former staff, ministers, generals, and servants. And then he appointed his successor in front of everyone. Would they believe it?

I think they would.

It would be weird. But they were there. They know what happened.

If the king – or really the king's ghost – called together his entire nation, and in front of everyone appointed his successor, no one would question it. How do you fool an entire nation?

Strange? Hard to believe? But it happened. How do you get an entire nation to lie?

Between two and three million Jews heard God speak at Mount Sinai. They heard what would become the text of the Ten Commandments: know God exists, don't bow down to idols, don't swear falsely, honor the Sabbath, honor your parents, don't kill, don't commit adultery, don't steal, don't bear false witness, and don't covet.

Did it happen? The Jews said it did. The national revelation at Mount Sinai was a transformative national experience. God spoke to the nation. The Torah was the word of God: dietary laws, limits on sexual activity, laws against marrying non-Jews, national taxes, ethical standards, strict observance of festivals, different standards of dress, expensive financial obligations, and a host of rituals and customs. Jews were destined to be different.

And subsequent Jewish history – history that goes back 3,300 years – starts with the national revelation. Each event is a link connected to the link before it: the conquest of Canaanite Israel, 800 years of settlement and war, exile in Babylon, near extinction in Persia, the re-conquest of Israel, the construction of a massive (and expensive) religious complex in Jerusalem, revolt and war against the Roman Empire, 2,000 years of exile and dispersion, victimization, persecution, oppression, pogroms, specific targeted attacks, outrageous accusations, and the return to the Jewish homeland. Mount Sinai was the event that got the ball rolling, started the process, and branded the Jewish nation a distinct and unique people. If it is a hoax, when did they make it up?

The national revelation at Mount Sinai is a historic claim. It is no different than any other claim in history. A nation experienced something – like the Romans at Carthage and New Yorkers on 9/11 – and that something changed the way they lived and how they thought of themselves.

Are you bothered because the claim is supernatural?

Supernatural shouldn't make a difference. If a nation claims an event – it doesn't matter if it is a war, a conquest, a great leader, a UFO, or a revelation of God – it happened. A nation is too big to lie. A group of two-to-three million people leaves a lot of room for dissent, politics, ambition, splinter groups, differences of opinion, and agendas. If they agree something happened. It happened. They may argue about details. Different people may describe things differently. But the event is a fact.

Take it one step further. The Torah claims:

> You might inquire about times long past, from the day that God created man on earth, [exploring] one end of heaven to the other. Has there ever been anything like this great thing or has anything like it been heard? Have a people ever heard the voice of God speaking from the midst of the fire as you have heard and survived?[106]

Think about this claim. It claims the national revelation at Mount Sinai was a once-in-history occurrence. It will never happen again. It also says no one else will make a similar claim.

Why not? Single witness and small group claims are weak. You don't believe your neighbor spoke to Elvis. You wouldn't trust a member of the People's Temple.

But national claims are strong.

You believe that the French Revolution, the Roman conquest of Egypt, and World War Two are historical facts.

If the Jewish people fabricated a national claim, other groups will fabricate a national claim too. Why not? A national claim trumps a small group or single witness claim. That is obvious. And if the Jews got away with it, why not claim the same thing?

Good question.

But look throughout history: the Torah was right. No other religion, cult, group, or sect claims God spoke to their entire group. None. Most trust a prophet. A few have a disciple or two. But that's it. No one else claims God spoke to an entire nation.

Why not? It is the best claim.

The answer is simple. Nations don't lie. They can't. And you can't claim a national revelation unless it really happened.

Take Islam as an example.

Mohammed wasn't stupid. He knew a national revelation was better proof than a single witness. And he lived in the middle-of-nowhere. (The Arabian Peninsula was hundreds of miles from civilization. The great world powers – the Eastern Roman and Persian Empires – were far away and busy fighting each other.) His followers were illiterate nomads. If anyone could fake a national revelation, it was Mohammed.[107]

Why didn't he?

Why didn't he say, "Remember when our ancestors stood together in Mecca and heard God's voice?"

Why didn't he do it? He didn't do it because you can't claim a national revelation unless it happened. Even an illiterate nomad knows that.

Why didn't Mohammed tell his followers, "Forget your ancestors; don't you remember when God spoke to us?"

Mohammed was a single witness. His followers believed him. He convinced them that God spoke to him. That he could do. But convincing them God spoke to *him* is different than convincing them that God spoke to *them*.

Imagine that we are talking.

I tell you to wait.

I walk into the bathroom. I lock the door.

And then something happens to me. The lights change color. The roof disappears. A large vacuum sucks me into the sky. I black out. I wake up on a spaceship. I am strapped to a bed. Aliens surround me. They are green. They have thousands of eyes. The prick me with needles, run tests, ask me questions I don't understand, and feed me foam.

They blast me light years across the universe. The spaceship lands on a planet called Zorkon. They stick me in a zoo. Years go by. I am famous. Zorkonian children visit the zoo, look at me, make funny faces, and feed me peanuts.

Zorkon is cold and smells like potatoes.

After 100 years, the Zorkonian Society for the Prevention of Cruelty to Animals takes over the planet. They close the zoo and send me home. They blast me light years back across the universe. They drop me in the bathroom I was abducted from.

It is two minutes later. You are waiting for me. I say, "You are not going to believe me. Aliens abducted me. I lived in a zoo on a planet called Zorkon."

Do you believe me?

Maybe. If you trust me, if I have evidence, or if I am a quick talker, I may be able to convince you that I was abducted by aliens. It would be hard. You are skeptical. But if I am persistent and my story doesn't change, you may believe me.

Could I convince you that aliens abducted you too? No. I can convince you that something happened to *me*. I can't convince you that something happened to *you*.

I could drug you, lock you in a box, torture you, abuse you, and then convince you.

Maybe.

But even if I could, could I drug, torture, manipulate, and psychologically abuse two-to-three million people?

Impossible.

Think about something else.

The Torah mandates two holidays – Passover and Shavuos – to commemorate the exodus and national revelation. Every year, every

Jewish family gets together for a special meal (the Seder). Every year – at the Seder – the family declares (out loud, so everyone can hear), "This is to remember that God took us out of Egypt." And then – fifty days later – they celebrate Shavuos. They eat cheesecake. They spend the night awake studying the Torah. In the morning, in synagogue, a community leader reads the story of the national revelation. He reads it out loud. Everyone stands up when he reaches the Ten Commandments.

If the claim is a hoax, when were these holidays introduced? Imagine the first Shavuos. Someone reads about the national revelation out loud. Someone else says, "I never heard this before."

Anarchy. Pandemonium. Bedlam. Mayhem. And the Torah says, "This is your history. Keep the commandments because your ancestors witnessed a national revelation." Really?

Believing the national revelation isn't irrelevant like believing the story about Caesar, Cleopatra, and the rug. It has serious implications: laws, history, restrictions, and being different. Would you be different based on something that never happened?

You can't fake a national experience. You believe that 9/11, the Holocaust, the Punic Wars, and Vietnam are facts of history. They were witnessed by millions of people. Nations don't lie. And unlike Caesar and Cleopatra, these events were important.

If you were God and you wanted a nation to follow your laws, you would tell the nation. You wouldn't pick a prophet and tell him in private. That would be as weak as an Elvis sighting.

The Jewish nation is the only nation that claims a national revelation. The national revelation is a fact of history. Nations can't lie. If they could, other nations would claim a national revelation as well.

Transmission: The Accuracy of the Torah's Transmission

Don't play devil's advocate. Pretend you agree. God spoke to the Jewish people at Mount Sinai. You bought the argument.

Great.

But how do you know the Torah didn't change? How do you know that the Torah is the same as it was when Moses gave it to the Jewish people?

The Torah was written a long time ago. A lot has happened since then. The Jews were exiled. They were persecuted. They wandered. Jewish communities span the globe, from Poland to Yemen to Chile to India to the United States. And they have not had a central religious authority since the Sanhedrin was dissolved about 2,000 years ago.

Were they able to maintain the accuracy of the Torah?

The Torah is a big book. It has 304,805 letters or about 79,000 words. It is written by hand. It is written on large pieces of animal skin. These sections are sewn together and assembled as a scroll. (Modern books are assembled in a format called a codex.)

When was the first complete Torah scroll written?

The Jewish people gathered at Mount Sinai in 1313 BCE. Moses died forty years later on February 23, 1273 BCE.[108] Before his death, he presented the nation with a completed copy of the Torah. This copy was kept in the Ark of the Covenant.[109]

Moses' Torah was the master copy. If someone was concerned about the accuracy of a scroll, he checked it against the master copy.

Each Jewish king was commanded to write a Torah scroll, too. It was a small scroll. He took it into battle. He kept it near him when he judged cases. He studied from it. And it was copied from the master copy that Moses wrote.[110] When the king died, his scroll was used as a master copy as well.

What happened to these scrolls?

The scroll written by Moses was kept in the Temple in Jerusalem. King Solomon built the Temple. The Babylonians sacked Jerusalem and destroyed the Temple in 422 BCE. Moses' master copy was either hidden away or destroyed at that time. The kings' copies disappeared over time as well.

But by then thousands of Torah scrolls had been written. Many scrolls were with the Jewish communities in Babylon (in modern day Iraq). Some of these scrolls were brought to Babylon years before the conquest and destruction of Jerusalem.

Moses' master copy was written 3,300 years ago and disappeared about a thousand years after that. That was a long time ago.

Or was it?

Every Torah scroll is copied from a master copy. Each master copy was copied from a master copy as well.

How many master copies do you need to get back to the one Moses wrote?

A Torah scroll can last a long time. I looked online. I found a 730-year-old Torah from Spain. A synagogue in Manhattan claimed their Torah was about 700-years-old, too. Many communities claim to have scrolls that are 400 or 500-years-old. The synagogue I grew up in had a Torah rescued from the Holocaust. The edges were burnt. It was at least 100-years-old.

Old Torah scrolls are not unusual.

The average life expectancy for a Torah scroll is about 200 years. Some last longer. Others don't. It depends on usage, quality of the parchment, climate, and other factors.

If the average Torah lasts for 200 years, how many master copies do you need to get back to Moses' master copy?

Not many.

Divide 3,000 years by 200 (the average life expectancy of a Torah scroll). You get fifteen. That's it. Only fifteen master copies back to Moses. If you want to get technical, Moses died in 1273 BCE. Add 200 years and one more scroll: sixteen.

Only sixteen scrolls back to Moses. That's nothing. And that is going back to when it was written. Moses' mastery copy didn't disappear until 422 BCE, about 2,400 years ago.

Or do the math; it is only *twelve* Torah scrolls back to the date that Moses' Torah disappeared.

And it isn't enough to copy a scroll from a master copy. The writing process is governed by a litany of laws, guidelines, and regulations.

It is difficult to write a Torah. You have to be trained. And you need to get certified. A scribe (*sofer*) is person certified to write a Torah. Certification as a scribe is similar to rabbinic ordination, getting certified to slaughter animals, or getting certified to perform circumcisions. You need to study. You need specific training. And you need to pass a test.

And the laws of writing a Torah are very exact. Twenty problems render a Torah unusable. If a defective Torah isn't corrected, it has to be discarded. Look at this partial list:[111]

- א It can't have one extra letter
- א It can't have one letter missing
- א The parchment, ink, and quill must conform to strict specifications. They must be prepared specifically for the purpose of writing a Torah scroll
- א The scribe cannot write from memory. Every letter must be copied from a master copy
- א The scribe must pronounce every word out loud before copying it from the master copy
- א Every letter must have sufficient white space surrounding it. If one letter touches another – in any spot – it invalidates the entire scroll
- א If a letter is unreadable or resembles another letter the scroll is invalid
- א The scribe must put precise space between words, so that one word will not look like two words, or two words like one word

‿ The scribe must not alter the design of the sections, and
 must conform to particular line-lengths and paragraph con-
 figurations

These laws help ensure the accuracy of the transmission. Writing a Torah is hard work. It requires training and dedication. It is
mandated by a strict set of rules. And these rules necessitate regular
maintenance and upkeep.

Take it a step further. The Torah isn't a secret document. It isn't
hidden in a vault. It is a communal object. Everyone reads from it
and sees it regularly.

And it is read in public.

Moses decreed that the Torah should be read in public once a
week. It is read every Shabbos morning. The weekly reading is called
a *parsha*. The Torah is divided into about fifty readings. It takes a
community one year to read the entire Torah, from start to finish.[112]
At the end of the year, they make a big party and start over again.

In the fourth century BCE, a group of Babylonian exiles returned
to Israel. They rebuilt the Temple in Jerusalem. They reestablished a
Jewish presence. And their leaders were Ezra and Nehemiah.

Ezra decreed that the Torah should be read in public three times a
week. This was in addition to the weekly reading established by Moses. Ezra's decree is still in effect. The Torah is read every Monday,
Thursday, and Shabbos afternoon. It is a much shorter reading, but
it means that each community's Torah scroll is in constant use. The
Torah is also read on holidays and fast days.

The Torah readings cannot be done from memory. The reader has
to look at every word he is reading.

Think about it. The Torah is in constant use. The person reading
it must look carefully at each word. If the scroll has a mistake, he is
going to find it.

What happens if he finds a mistake?

The scroll is considered defective. It must be corrected within
thirty days. If it isn't corrected, it must be discarded.

Did you ever see the reader find a mistake?

He stops reading. He asks the rabbi to take a look. The rabbi calls
over an expert. They discuss it.

And a mistake can be anything; a missing or extra letter, a smudge,
an unusual shape, or two letters that look connected.

If they decide it's a mistake, they roll up the Torah, fasten the Torah's belt over the outer cover, and put it away. It is a red flag when the belt is fastened over the outer cover. It alerts the community that this Torah needs to be repaired. It looks funny because the belt is usually under the Torah's outer covering to keep the scroll from unraveling.

Incredible.

Every Torah scroll is written from a master copy. Moses wrote the original master copy. His copy is only sixteen Torahs away. The laws of writing a Torah are very exact. The Torah is in constant use. It is read in public. It is corrected or discarded if it is defective. And it is not a secret document. Everyone has access to it. Everyone gets to see it. Most people are called up to read from the Torah a few times a year.

And many people travel. They visit other communities. They visit other synagogues. They read from other scrolls. And when people move to new communities, they bring their old scrolls with them.

Torah scrolls are examined, checked, compared, referenced, and crosschecked all the time. Every scroll is seen multiple times by many different people.

Add up these factors. The Jewish people have a lot of safeguards in place to ensure an accurate transmission.

But so what.

Did it work? Was the Torah accurately transmitted?

Rabbi Mordechai Breuer was a contemporary Bible scholar. He won the Israel Prize, Israel's highest honor. He was an expert concerning the accuracy of the Bible's text. Many people consider his edition of the Hebrew Bible the most accurate edition.[113]

Rabbi Breuer did a comprehensive analysis of the Torah's text. He compared four ancient texts written in different parts of the world. He also included a fifth text, a 16th century edition printed in Italy. Using a sophisticated method, he isolated differences, identified copyists' errors, and established an authoritative model.

Rabbi Breuer compared his model with Torah scrolls from Yemen. Why Yemen? Yemenite Jews were isolated. Yemen was remote. It was far away from other Jewish communities. It was an old community. It was physically separated from other communities for about 2,000 years. They were isolated, insular, small, and ancient. And for these reasons, experts consider Torahs from Yemen to be the most accurate.

The Torah contains 304,805 letters. When Rabbi Breuer compared his authoritative model with the Yemenite scrolls, he found nine letters in disagreement.[114]

That's it. Nine letters.[115]

Which nine letters?

All nine were alternate spellings. None changed the meaning of the text. None had theological implications. The differences were similar to differences in spelling between America and England.

For example, in America, color is spelled COLOR. In England it is spelled COLOUR. It is the same word. It means the same thing. In England it has a U. In America it doesn't. The difference is meaningless.

The nine letter differences were similar. They were insignificant.

And the nine differences were probably copyist errors. These errors were in the original Torahs brought by the Jews who first moved to Yemen.[116]

That is an amazing stat.

The Torah is about 3,300 years old. Despite wandering, exile, and persecution, the Torah's text was preserved with amazing accuracy. Out of 304,805 letters, only nine letters are in disagreement. And those nine discrepancies are insignificant.

How does that stat compare with other ancient religious texts?

Compare the Torah to the New Testament as an example.

The New Testament is about the same length as the Torah. It was written about 1,300 years later. It is younger. And for much of its history, Christianity had the Vatican – a central governing authority. The Vatican could supervise the transmission, manage the text, and prevent inaccuracies and variant versions. The Christians were not persecuted for most of their history. They were never exiled.

Jews wander. Christians don't.

How did they do? How accurate was the transmission of the New Testament?

Look at this quote from the *Interpreter's Dictionary of the Bible*, a 5-volume research guide written for pastors and seminary students:

A study of 150 Greek [manuscripts] of the Gospel of Luke has revealed more than 30,000 different readings... It is safe to say that there is not one sentence in the New Testament in which the [manuscript] is wholly uniform.[117]

Josh McDowell is an evangelist. His book, *Evidence that Demands a Verdict*, is listed number thirteen in the top fifty list of evangelical books.[118] As evidence in support of the New Testament, he reported:

> There are some 200,000 variants in the existing manuscripts of the New Testament, representing about 400 variant readings which cause doubt about textual meaning; 50 of these are of great significance.[119]

How does the Torah compare to the New Testament?

The Torah is 3,300 years old. It has 304,805 letters. It has nine letters where the original sequencing is in doubt. The nine discrepancies are insignificant.

The New Testament is about 2,000 years old. It has 200,000 variant readings. It has 400 instances that change the meaning of the text. And fifty of those are of great significance.

The point is not to denigrate the New Testament. The point is to show how difficult it is to preserve the integrity of an ancient text.

Do your homework. Examine the accuracy of other ancient religious books. How did they do?

The accurate transmission of the Torah is unusual. And it is amazing. Is it perfect?

No.

But it is close.

Control

Esther, Purim, and the Nazis

Pretend I want to impress you. I tell you it will rain on Tuesday. It happens. It rains on Tuesday. Are you impressed? Probably not.

I tell you it will rain on Thursday at 10:03. It happens. It rains on Thursday at 10:03. Now are you impressed? Maybe. But maybe I got lucky.

I tell you it will rain on Sunday at 9:41 for exactly 13 minutes. The rain will be very heavy. It will stop after 13 minutes and the sun will shine as if nothing happened.

It happens. It rains on Sunday at 9:41 for exactly 13 minutes, the rain is very heavy, it stops, and the sun shines as if nothing happened.

Wow.

How did I do it? Maybe I am a witch. Maybe I own a weather machine. Maybe I seeded the clouds. I don't want to tell you. But I control the weather and you are impressed. Amazing.

That is an example of specific control. I controlled events to work out the way I wanted them to and I predicted what would happen in advance.

What about the Bible? Does it contain an example of specific control? Did God or a prophet predict a specific event and it happened?

Take a look.

Amalek was an ancient nation. They hated Jews. They attacked when the Jews were about to settle the land of Israel. And they didn't just attack. They tried to kill every Jewish man, woman, and child. They were ruthless.

Amalek attacked the Jews three times throughout history. They attacked in ancient times, when the Jews were wandering in the desert and about to settle the Land of Israel for the first time. They attacked about 800 years later, in the days of the Persian exile, when the Jews were preparing to return to Israel and rebuild Jerusalem. And they attacked in Nazi Germany, during World War Two, when the Jews were about to establish the modern Israeli state.

Well maybe.

It depends. Were the Nazis Amalek? If they were, it is a cute paradigm. Amalek attacked three times – each time before the Jews were about to settle in Israel – and they were ruthless. If the bible makes a specific reference to the Nazis, it is an example of specific control. Were they Amalek?

What is Amalek? What did they stand for?

Look at this quote. It is from Rabbi Tzadok HaCohen, a famous Hasidic rabbi from the 1800s:

1. In a man's heart, Amalek is the power that "freezes" man, causing him to see only "absurd chance" and therefore deny an ethical conscience and the moral perfection it entails.
2. In the physical body, Amalek fights to destroy the sanctity of Bris Mila – the Covenant of Circumcision.
3. In space, Amalek covets the Land of Israel, and is sworn to prevent Israel from attaining its perfection – which is interdependent with its dwelling in the Land.
4. In the history of Mankind, Amalek symbolizes the "foremost evil among the nations."[120]

Based on this definition, Amalek is four things. Amalek hates ethics and morality. Amalek hates circumcision. Amalek attacks when the Jews are poised to establish a presence in Israel. And Amalek is evil.

Does that definition fit the Nazis?

Look at this quote. It is from Hermann Rauschning. Rauschning was a conservative German politician from Danzig. He joined the left wing National Socialists in 1932. He fled Germany in 1936 and resigned his post in the Danzig senate. He claimed to have had hundreds of conversations with Hitler during his years as a Nazi. In the late 1930s he published a number of books based on those conversations.[121]

> Hitler stated: It is true. We are barbarians. It is an honorable title. I free humanity from the shackles of the soul, from the degrading suffering caused by a false vision called conscience and morality.
>
> The Jews have inflicted two wounds on mankind – circumcision on its body and conscience on its soul. These are Jewish inventions.
>
> The war for world domination will be fought entirely between us — the Germans and the Jews. All else is façade and illusion.[122]

Based on the definition from Rabbi Tzadok and these quotes from Hitler, the Nazis fit the definition of Amalek. They hated ethics and morality. They hated circumcision. They attacked when the Jews were preparing to establish a state in Israel. And they were evil.

Great. Are you impressed? Probably not. It is an interesting parallel, but it doesn't show specific control.

Look at this quote from the Talmud.

> Rav Yitzhak said: What is meant by the verse (Psalms 140:9), "Oh God, don't grant the desires of the evil man, and don't let him draw out his bit, lest he raise himself above the others."
>
> Jacob our forefather said to God: "Don't grant the desires of the evil man" – this refers to Esau. "And don't let him draw out his bit" – this refers to Germamia of Edom, for should the go forth they would destroy the entire world.[123]

Consider a few facts. The Talmud is old. It was edited and reedited, but completed by the year 500 of the Common Era. It was written in modern day Iraq. It was written in Aramaic. And it pre-dates most post-Roman European history. The Talmud discusses Jewish law and explains the deeper meaning of many biblical verses.

Think about the quote above. The Talmud cites a verse from the Book of Psalms. It tells you what the verse means: it is a prayer by Jacob on behalf of future generations. So far so good.

But that is where it gets weird. According to the Talmud, Jacob was worried about Germamia. Germamia is *Germany*.[124]

Does that make sense?

In the year 500, Jews were worried about Romans, Byzantines, and Persians. Germany was a nonentity. The German people were uncivilized barbarians. Why was the Talmud worried about a nation that didn't exist?

Specifically, the Talmud claimed that Jacob asked God, 'Not to remove Germany's bit.' A bit is a piece of metal or hard wood that fits in a horse's mouth. The bit is attached to reins. The rider controls the horse by pulling the bit. If the bit is loose, the horse does what it wants.

Jacob asked God to hold Germany back. He wanted the bit in Germany's mouth. He didn't want them to run wild.

What was the bit? What held them back? The Talmud continues:

> Rebbe Chama bar Chanina said: There are 300 crowned princes in Germamia of Edom and 365 chieftains in Rome, and every day one goes out to meet the other, and one of them is killed – and they all have the trouble of appointing a king again.

The bit was German disunity. Germany had 300 crowned princes. Each one ruled a mini-kingdom. They hated each other. And as long as the Germans were fighting each other, they couldn't cause trouble elsewhere.

The Talmud's number was specific, too. It mentioned 300 crowned princes. Look at this quote:

> By the end of the Middle Ages, which had seen Britain and France emerge as unified nations, Germany remained a crazy patchwork of some three hundred individual states.[125]

Think about it. By the end of the Middle Ages most of Europe was conquering the world. Britain, France, Spain, Portugal, and the Dutch had built massive colonial empires. But not the Germans. Germany couldn't get out of Central Europe. They were too busy fighting each other.

But after a long series of events, on January 18, 1871, Otto Von Bismarck proclaimed the unification of the German Empire at the Hall of Mirrors in Versailles.[126]

And what happened next?

Trouble. World War I, World War II, the Holocaust – German unification was trouble for the world and terrible for the Jews. The Talmud was right.

Specific. And it is a stronger example of control than the Nazis fitting Rabbi Tzadok's definition of Amalek.

But is there an even more specific example?

Take a look at the Book of Esther (it tells the Purim story). Chapter nine has a page that looks like this:

ויכו היהודים בכל איביהם מכת חרב והרג ואבדן ויעשו בשנאיהם
כרצונם: ובשושן הבירה הרגו היהודים ואבד חמש מאות איש: ואת

ואת	פַּרְשַׁנְדָּתָא
ואת	דַּלְפוֹן
ואת	אַסְפָּתָא
ואת	פּוֹרָתָא
ואת	אֲדַלְיָא
ואת	אֲרִידָתָא
ואת	פַּרְמַשְׁתָּא
ואת	אֲרִיסַי
ואת	אֲרִידַי
עֲשֶׂרֶת	וַיְזָתָא

בְּנֵי הָמָן בֶּן הַמְּדָתָא צֹרֵר הַיְּהוּדִים הָרָגוּ וּבַבִּזָּה לֹא שָׁלְחוּ אֶת יָדָם:
בַּיּוֹם הַהוּא בָּא מִסְפַּר הַהֲרוּגִים בְּשׁוּשַׁן הַבִּירָה לִפְנֵי הַמֶּלֶךְ: וַיֹּאמֶר
הַמֶּלֶךְ לְאֶסְתֵּר הַמַּלְכָּה בְּשׁוּשַׁן הַבִּירָה הָרְגוּ הַיְּהוּדִים וְאַבֵּד חֲמֵשׁ
מֵאוֹת אִישׁ וְאֵת עֲשֶׂרֶת בְּנֵי הָמָן בִּשְׁאָר מְדִינוֹת הַמֶּלֶךְ מֶה עָשׂוּ
וּמַה שְּׁאֵלָתֵךְ וְיִנָּתֵן לָךְ וּמַה בַּקָּשָׁתֵךְ עוֹד וְתֵעָשׂ: וַתֹּאמֶר אֶסְתֵּר אִם
עַל הַמֶּלֶךְ טוֹב יִנָּתֵן גַּם מָחָר לַיְּהוּדִים אֲשֶׁר בְּשׁוּשַׁן לַעֲשׂוֹת כְּדָת
הַיּוֹם וְאֵת עֲשֶׂרֶת בְּנֵי הָמָן יִתְלוּ עַל הָעֵץ: וַיֹּאמֶר הַמֶּלֶךְ לְהֵעָשׂוֹת
כֵּן וַתִּנָּתֵן דָּת בְּשׁוּשָׁן וְאֵת עֲשֶׂרֶת בְּנֵי הָמָן תָּלוּ:

This page is always written the same way, as two columns in a larger font. The laws are very exact. Every copy has to be the same.

The Book of Esther is an unusual biblical book. It never mentions God. You expect the bible to talk about God – and it does – except for the Book of Esther.

The Book of Esther is a code for future generations. It is one of the last books of the bible. The end of the bible is the end of prophecy. But God didn't disappear with prophecy, He is just harder to find. The Book of Esther tells you where to look. If the text mentions King Achashverosh, it is referring to King Achashverosh. That much is obvious. But if it mentions just the "King" – and not "King Achashverosh" – it is referring to the King of Kings, i.e. God. God is in the story, but He is hidden.

This is a translation of the page from the Book of Esther I mentioned above. It is a conversation between Esther and the "King." Read it carefully. Do you notice anything weird?

> And the Jews struck at all their enemies with the sword, and with slaughter and destruction, and they did as they pleased to those who hated them. And in Shushan the capital, the Jews slew and destroyed five hundred men, including Parshandasa, and Dalphon, and Aspasa, and Porasa, and Adalia, and Aridasa, and Parmashta, and Arisai, and Aridai, and Vaizasa, the ten sons of Haman, son of Hammedasa, the enemy of the Jews. But they did not lay their hands on the spoils.
>
> That same day the number of those killed in Shushan the capital was reported to the King. The King said to Queen Esther, "In Shushan the capital the Jews have slain and destroyed five hundred men including the ten sons of Haman; what have they done in the rest of the King's providences! What is your request now? It shall be granted to you. What is your petition further? It shall be fulfilled?"
>
> Esther replied, "If it pleases the King, allow the Jews of Shushan to do tomorrow as they have done today, and let Haman's ten sons be hanged on the gallows."
>
> The King ordered that this be done...

Did you catch it? Esther asked the King to hang Haman's ten sons. Do you see the problem?

They were already dead.

Read it again. Do you see it? Esther asked the king to hang ten dead men.

Weird.

Why would she do that? Keep in mind that she was speaking to the King – not King Achashverosh. Was she speaking to God? If so, why didn't she ask for something big like world peace or the messianic era? Why did she ask God to hang ten dead men?

One thing to consider, Esther asked the King to hang them "tomorrow." Tomorrow means, "tomorrow" – i.e. the day after today. But it also means "tomorrow" in the poetic sense, as in the future.

Interesting.

In 1946, ten Nazis were hung in Nuremberg, Germany. They were the masterminds of the Holocaust. They were sentenced to death at the conclusion of the Nuremberg War Crimes Trials. Eleven Nazis were convicted in June 1946. Hermann Göring — a leading Nazi and close associate of Hitler — killed himself in prison. The other ten were hung on October 16, 1946.

1946 was the Hebrew year 5706, at least until Rosh Hashanah – the Jewish New Year. After Rosh Hashanah the year changed to 5707. Rosh Hashanah in 1946 was on September 26. The ten Nazis were hung after Rosh Hashanah, on October 16, in 5707.

Hebrew years are notated with letters, not numbers. That is not unusual. Before the invention of Arabic numerals, many cultures used letters to represent numerical values. Hebrew is similar. Each letter has a corresponding value. You are probably familiar with Roman numerals: i=1, v=5, x=10. Hebrew has a similar system; each letter also represents a number.

I am writing this in 5770. The calendar on my wall notes it with the Hebrew letters "Tav," "Shin," "Ayin." In Hebrew it looks like this: תש"ע

In October 1946, the Hebrew year was 5707. It looked like this: תש"ז

Look carefully at the letters:

✡ Tav – ת

✡ Shin – ש

✡ Zion – ז

Below is the list of Haman's ten sons from the Book of Esther. It is from the same page in chapter nine noted above. Look carefully at the first, seventh, and last names. Do you see three letters printed in a smaller font than the others? I circled them to make them easy to find.

Coincidence?

ויכו היהודים בכל איביהם מכת חרב והרג ואבדן ויעשו בשנאיהם
כרצונם: ובשושן הבירה הרגו היהודים ואבד חמש מאות איש: ואת

ואת	פרשנדתא
ואת	דלפון
ואת	אספתא
ואת	פורתא
ואת	אדליא
ואת	ארידתא
ואת	פרמשתא
ואת	אריסי
ואת	ארידי
עשרת	ויזתא

בני המן בן המדתא צרר היהודים הרגו ובבזה לא שלחו את ידם:
ביום ההוא בא מספר ההרוגים בשושן הבירה לפני המלך: ויאמר
המלך לאסתר המלכה בשושן הבירה הרגו היהודים ואבד חמש
מאות איש ואת עשרת בני המן בשאר מדינות המלך מה עשו
ומה שאלתך וינתן לך ומה בקשתך עוד ותעש: ותאמר אסתר אם
על המלך טוב ינתן גם מחר ליהודים אשר בשושן לעשות כדת
היום ואת עשרת בני המן יתלו על העץ: ויאמר המלך להעשות
כן ותנתן דת בשושן ואת עשרת בני המן תלו:

Esther asked God to hang Haman's sons a second time. She asked Him to do it tomorrow, i.e. in the future.

The Nazis fit the definition of Amalek. The Talmud warned about German unification. And Esther asked God to repeat the conclusion of the Purim story.

And she was exact. In her book – the Book of Esther – she indicated that this repeat was to take place in 5707. How did she do it? She hid three little letters in her list of defeated enemies.

Keep in mind that Jewish law is very exact, especially when it comes to writing holy books. Scribes follow a specific set of rules. They know when to make a break in a column or a break in a line, when to write a letter in a smaller font, and when to write a letter in a larger font. A Book of Esther written before World War Two has the same little letters as one written today.

Spooky.

But there is a problem. Add up the value of Tav, Shin, and Zion:

- Tav = 400
- Shin = 300
- Zion = 7

That only adds up to 707. Why?

Tav is the last letter in the Hebrew alphabet. Its value is 400. To write a number as big as 5,000, you need a lot of Tavs. It is too cumbersome. When indicating years, Hebrew uses a type of shorthand and it leaves out the thousands column. In most cases, that is good enough. The Hebrew year is written on legal contracts, bills of sale, and religious documents. Most people know the millennium they are living in and the system works.

But if Esther is going to hint at a repeat of the Purim story, she needs to be exact. She has to indicate the millennium in addition to the particular year. Otherwise, which 707 is she referring to? Maybe she meant 4707.

What millennium is 5707? Count:

- 707=one
- 1707=two
- 2707=three
- 3707=four

ℵ 4707=five

ℵ 5707=six

5707 is the sixth millennium. It is the sixth appearance of 707. What Hebrew letter has a value of 6? It is Vav, ו.

Vav = 6.

Look carefully at what Vav looks like – ו.

On the following page is the list of Haman's ten sons from the Book of Esther again. It is from the same page in chapter nine noted above. Look at the last name listed. Do you see a letter that is bigger than the others? I circled it to make it easy to find (following page).

The large Vav indicates the millennium. The execution was repeated in the sixth millennium.

Or 5707 to be exact.

Esther wasn't close. She indicated *exactly* when the story would be repeated. And it happened.

The Nazis were hung on October 16. In 5707, October 16 was Hoshanah Rabbah. Hoshanah Rabba is a Jewish holiday. It is the last day of the Succos festival. According to Jewish tradition, Hoshanah Rabbah is judgment day for non-Jews. Jews are judged on Rosh Hashanah. They get a second chance on Yom Kippur. And the non-Jews are judged on Hoshanah Rabbah.

Interesting.

Hermann Göring — one of the Nazis sentenced to death at the Nuremberg Trials – committed suicide. In the Purim story, Haman's daughter committed suicide. According to Albert Speer — Hitler's architect and a close confidant — Göring was a cross-dresser. He wore women's clothing at home and women's underwear under his military uniform.[127]

Think about it. Haman had eleven children. Ten sons were hung and his daughter committed suicide. Eleven Nazis were convicted. Ten were hung and the cross-dresser committed suicide.

Impressive. And a great example of specific control. It doesn't get any better.

Or does it?

What if the Nazis, as they were being executed, said that it was Purim all over again? Imagine if they claimed their execution was a repeat of the Purim story. That would be amazing.

Take a look.

On October 28, 1946, Newsweek magazine published an article about the executions. The article described the executions of each Nazi and noted his last words. Look at how Newsweek described the hanging of Julius Streicher, publisher of *Der Stürmer* newspaper and an important Nazi propagandist:

ויכו היהודים בכל איביהם מכת חרב והרג ואבדן ויעשו בשנאיהם
כרצונם: ובשושן הבירה הרגו היהודים ואבד חמש מאות איש: ואת

ואת	פַּרְשַׁנְדָּתָא
ואת	דַּלְפוֹן
ואת	אַסְפָּתָא
ואת	פּוֹרָתָא
ואת	אֲדַלְיָא
ואת	אֲרִידָתָא
ואת	פַּרְמַשְׁתָּא
ואת	אֲרִיסַי
ואת	אֲרִידַי
עֲשֶׂרֶת	וַיְזָתָא

בְּנֵי הָמָן בֶּן הַמְּדָתָא צֹרֵר הַיְּהוּדִים הָרָגוּ וּבַבִּזָּה לֹא שָׁלְחוּ אֶת יָדָם:
בַּיּוֹם הַהוּא בָּא מִסְפַּר הַהֲרוּגִים בְּשׁוּשַׁן הַבִּירָה לִפְנֵי הַמֶּלֶךְ: וַיֹּאמֶר
הַמֶּלֶךְ לְאֶסְתֵּר הַמַּלְכָּה בְּשׁוּשַׁן הַבִּירָה הָרְגוּ הַיְּהוּדִים וְאַבֵּד חֲמֵשׁ
מֵאוֹת אִישׁ וְאֵת עֲשֶׂרֶת בְּנֵי הָמָן בִּשְׁאָר מְדִינוֹת הַמֶּלֶךְ מֶה עָשׂוּ
וּמַה שְּׁאֵלָתֵךְ וְיִנָּתֵן לָךְ וּמַה בַּקָּשָׁתֵךְ עוֹד וְתֵעָשׂ: וַתֹּאמֶר אֶסְתֵּר אִם
עַל הַמֶּלֶךְ טוֹב יִנָּתֵן גַּם מָחָר לַיְּהוּדִים אֲשֶׁר בְּשׁוּשָׁן לַעֲשׂוֹת כְּדָת
הַיּוֹם וְאֵת עֲשֶׂרֶת בְּנֵי הָמָן יִתְלוּ עַל הָעֵץ: וַיֹּאמֶר הַמֶּלֶךְ לְהֵעָשׂוֹת
כֵּן וַתִּנָּתֵן דָּת בְּשׁוּשָׁן וְאֵת עֲשֶׂרֶת בְּנֵי הָמָן תָּלוּ:

Only Julius Streicher went without dignity. He had to be pushed across the floor, wild-eyed and screaming: "Heil Hitler!" Mounting the steps he cried out: "And now I go to God." He stared at the witnesses facing the gallows and shouted **"Purim-fest 1946."** (Purim is a Jewish feast.)[128]

That is control. And it is specific. The Nazis said so themselves.

What Do You Think?

The Torah is the most important Jewish book.

Everything Jewish is in it: Jewish values, ethics, morals, history, holidays, traditions, and laws. It is influential. It is not the outdated epic of an ancient people. It is alive and well. And many people think that God wrote it.

What do you think?

You saw five classes of evidence. Each class was a piece in a puzzle. Put the pieces together. Did they add up? Was the evidence compelling?

Think about each class of evidence.

Outside Verification: Jewish history doesn't make sense. It is weird, contradictory, unique, and counter-intuitive. Enlightened writers like Mark Twain, Leo Tolstoy, and John Adams took notice. They were impressed. And they wrote about it.

The unusual, unique history of the Jewish people was written in the Torah – at least 2,000 years ago – before any of it happened. The Torah was explicit. It warned the Jewish people about their destiny in clear, unambiguous language. The claims were made at the start of Jewish history – before the Jews did anything – and the Torah was right. The claims and contradictions happened the way it said they would.

How do you explain that?

Codes: The Torah is chockful of words and ideas hidden as equidistant letter skips. Are these skips a fluke or were they encoded by design? The odds that it was fluke are 1 in 1,694,000.

Interesting.

Does the phenomenon occur in every large book?

No. The codes researchers ran one million tests; the phenomenon is exclusive to the Torah.

Did the Jews hide equidistant letter sequences about the future when they were wandering in the desert?

Maybe.

But does that make sense?

Identifying Information: The Torah listed only one animal – the pig – that chews its cud but doesn't have split hooves. The Torah indicated that the pig is the only animal like this.

And it was right.

Was Moses a Zoologist? How did he know?

Transmission: The Jewish people claimed a national revelation at Mount Sinai. They were the only nation in history to claim a national revelation.

Nations can't lie.

If they could, why didn't other nations claim a national revelation, too?

And the Torah was accurately transmitted. The Torah is 3,300 years old. It has 304,805 letters. It only has nine in disagreement. And the nine discrepancies are insignificant.

How do explain that?

Control: How did Esther know that the Purim story would be repeated in 5707? How did she get it right?

And who put "Purimfest" in Julius Streicher's mouth?

What do you think?

Is the evidence compelling? I think it is. Is it foolproof? No. But do you have to take a leap of faith?

Absolutely not.

If you knew this much information about a house you wanted to buy, would you buy it?

I think you would.

If an auto mechanic showed you this much evidence about a noise your car was making, would you let him fix it?

Yes. I think you would.

If you knew this much evidence about a job you wanted or a person you wanted to marry, would you do it?

Of course you would. Most people do it for less.

Is this enough evidence to believe that God wrote the Torah?

I think it is.

But you can answer that for yourself.

Appendix

Torah Codes: Responding to the Critics

By Rabbi Moshe Zeldman

Scientific research has confirmed that there are hidden codes in the Torah[1]. Given the consequences of this research, it was inevitable that some people would take exception to the findings. Despite the integrity of the research and the researchers, critics have made many strong attempts to refute the research and discredit the researchers.[2]

We are not under any illusion that any counter-arguments will have any effect on the critics. For most of them, the issue is not the *existence* of codes; it's the *implication*, which runs contrary to their a priori assumptions about the divinity of the Torah. This view is best expressed by one of the critics. When challenged, "What evidence would be enough to convince you that the codes exist?" She responded, "*No* amount of evidence. I *know* that the Torah was written by human beings." For other reasons, even religious Jews can be ideologically bothered by the idea that the Torah has such hidden codes.

Scientific evidence rests on facts, demonstrated through repeated experimentation and independent verification. This has been done, and is the basis of our reliance on the authenticity of Torah codes. We present here some of the most common misconceptions and claims made by the various critics, as well as our responses.

Myth #1:

Scientists have disproven the idea of codes in the Torah

Fact:

Statistical Science recently published an article in which the authors claim to have "solved the bible code puzzle." In truth, this article is a compilation of criticisms that have *helped* make the integrity of the Torah codes stronger than ever. At best, the critics have only raised questions of *possible* flaws in *one* of the early experiments.

The main point of the attack by the critics is the input data of the original Rabbis experiment of 1994 (see details below). The data was of a relatively complex nature, and was provided by an expert, Prof. S.Z. Havlin of Bar Ilan University, who is an internationally known scholar in the area of rabbinical bibliography. The critics, however, claim there is "wiggle room" in the data. Their arguments are riddled with logical, procedural and grammatical errors. But aside from these, *several* recent codes experiments have been conducted which completely avoid the need for any expert opinion for the input data. The data collection is simple and explicit and leaves no room for choices or optimization.

Myth #2:

The idea of Torah codes is not supported by Jewish tradition

Fact:

While there are even Rabbis who repeat this assertion, one would do well to look carefully at traditional and widely accepted Jewish sources that deal with the idea. The concept of "encoded information" and a "hidden text" in the Torah is a well-known and established part of Jewish tradition. The Ramban (Nachmanides), Maharal, the Vilna Gaon, and others refer to "hidden information in the letters of the Torah" in their writings. There are sources that *explicitly* state that such codes do exist in the Torah. In other words, the existence of codes in the Torah is not something new. All that is new is the ability to find them with computers and evaluate them with modern statistical methods. (See Section A below for more details.)

The critics then turn to the issue of rabbinic endorsement for codes research.

On March 2, 1997 the renowned Rabbi Shlomo Fisher testified that one of the greatest sages of our generation, Rabbi Shlomo Zalman Auerbach, met with the researchers on several occasions, issued a public statement in Jerusalem. He stated that Rabbi Auerbach not only gave his approval to

Codes research but also encouraged its use in Jewish educational venues. Rabbi Fisher is also familiar with the research, and wrote his own letters of encouragement.

More recently, several other leading Rabbis have given written endorsements regarding the validity of codes research, the integrity of the researchers, and have endorsed its presentation to lay audiences. (See Section B below for more details.)

Myth #3:

Scientists have disproved the existence of Torah codes by showing that such codes exist in other books, like *War and Peace* and *Moby Dick*.

Fact:

For anybody familiar with the basic idea of ELS codes (see Section C below for a simplified explanation), it is self-evident that one can find ELSs of words in any text. One could easily find "encoded words" on the side of a box of cereal, in this paragraph, and yes, even in *Moby Dick*. The question is not one of finding ELSs. **The simple fact is that no critic has found, or even claims to find, the statistically significant effect found in Genesis.** I.e. no critic has succeeded in taking an *objective* list of pairs of words, and shown that their ELSs appear near each other any more often than what would be expected in a comparably long text.

So what have the critics found? That theoretically one could cheat. I.e. that by surreptitiously *not* using an objective list of pairs of words, or by playing around with many alternative spellings of words, or by breaking basic rules of grammar, or by not considering minimal ELSs (see Section C below), one could concoct a contrived list and deceive people into believing that an objective experiment was performed.

This is precisely the method used by the critics to create counterfeit codes in *Moby Dick*; this is also the technique used in most of the popular books on Bible Codes, as well as the plethora of Christian codes books claiming that "Jesus is Messiah."

The only difference between the scientists opposed to codes, and the non-scientific use of codes (Michael Drosnin and the Christians) is that *the critics admit that their results were obtained through selective choices of data, i.e. cheating.* Their claim however, is that the original codes researchers cheated in this same way.

To summarize, there are no scientists who claim that hidden codes actually exist in different texts. Their claim is the opposite- that in fact, there is no such thing as a codes phenomenon in *any* text, and that the experiments performed and published are fraudulent.

See Myth #5 for the researchers' response to this claim.

Myth #4:

There is too much wiggle room (i.e. flexibility) in the experiments to consider them as objective science

Fact:

Ironically, when the critics first made this claim, they provided several instances of where the researchers could have "wiggled", involving certain choices of names, spellings of Hebrew dates, etc. When these apparent optimizations were examined by rerunning the original experiment, **the original results changed from a significance level of 16/1,000,000[3] to 4/1,000,000.** (See www.torahcodes.co.il/docum4eng.htm for more information).

In addition, one of the main questions regarding codes experiments is in the integrity of the data set, i.e. the set of words being searched for in the text. Doron Witztum and Professor Eliyahu Rips, the original researchers who conducted the Rabbis experiment, were well aware of this factor. To avoid any accusation of cheating, the task of deciding on spellings and constructing the list was delegated to an outside expert in rabbinical bibliography, Professor Shlomo Zalman Havlin, from the Faculty of Information Studies and Bibliography at Bar Ilan University[4]. Professor Havlin also pre-established a list of guidelines that would guide his determination of which forms and spellings of names he would take. The appellations used by the researchers were precisely those submitted to them by Professor Havlin.

When the critics questioned Professor Havlin about his methodology in establishing the list of names, he presented to them the guidelines he followed, Of course, when presented with this list of guidelines, the critics responded by claiming that he too must have been involved in the grand conspiracy! (His guidelines are available at www.torahcodes.co.il/havlin.htm.)

To further bolster their claim of wiggle room, the critics, through many months of experimenting with different combinations of appellations and spellings, fabricated their own list (which they admitted was doctored), which does succeed in the Hebrew translation of War and Peace. Their list, however, is riddled with spelling errors, data taken from inaccurate or ambiguous sources, and, despite their insistence to the contrary, repeatedly breaks the original guidelines set by Havlin. A full 45-page refutation of every one of their inadmissible choices is available at www.torahcodes.co.il/debate.htm.

Their response?

To find an "expert" to back up their claim that their list was valid and accurate. The one expert they managed to find was Professor Menachem Cohen, a professor of *Bible Studies* at Bar Ilan University.

Is there any reason to think that a Professor of Bible Studies could proffer an expert opinion on rabbinical bibliographic data any more than a professor of Chemistry, or a professor of English?[5]

For a sample of the many errors in their list, see Section D below.

Myth #5:

The researchers who conducted the Famous Rabbis experiment (published in Statistical Science in 1994) cheated by intentionally manipulating the data while conducting the experiment

Fact:

This claim has already been refuted from a number of angles.

A) Independent Verification

A number of independent researchers have confirmed the integrity of the data and methodology of the original experiment. Harold Gans, formerly a senior mathematician and cryptologist at the U.S. Dept. of Defense, conducted an independent experiment to verify the integrity of the data. He did so by searching for codes related to the <u>places</u> of birth and death corresponding to the precise listing of Rabbis used by Witztum and Rips. He obtained highly statistically significant results. The critics' response? Yes, he too must have somehow been involved in the (ever-growing) conspiracy.[6]

Furthermore, Israeli mathematician Alex Lubotsky challenge the researchers by speculating why they didn't run their experiment with a much simpler data set, composed of the names of the Rabbis the way they are referred to in Jewish tradition "so-and-so son of so-and-so". Witztum took the offer as a legitimate question, ran exactly such an experiment, and achieved significant results! Note that this experiment was a) suggested by one of the critics, and b) has no wiggle room.

In addition, Dr. Robert Haralick, Boeing Professor of Electrical Engineering and an expert in Pattern Recognition at the University of Washington, has confirmed the statistical significance of the original Great Rabbis experiment by rerunning the experiment using an entirely different methodology.

B) New Experiments

Many other experiments, including those by independent researchers, have further confirmed the existence of codes in the Torah. In brief:

a. Dr. Alex Rotenberg, a technical programmer in Jerusalem, conducted his own experiment looking for pairings of the names of the children of Haman (found in the Book of Esther 9:7-9) with their date of death, and obtained highly significant results. His experiment can be found at www.math.tau.ac.il/~tsirel/claims.htm.

b. Doron Witztum has recently conducted another new successful experiment, modeled after the original Rabbis experiment, searching for the names of personalities mentioned in Genesis (Adam, Isaac, the children of Jacob), and finding that they appear in proximity to their dates of birth. The beauty of this experiment is the lack of even potential "wiggle room". The data is taken directly from a Midrash, and the names are spelled exactly as they are found in the Book of Genesis. This experiment, as well as others, can be found at www.torahcodes.co.il/researches.htm.[7]

c. Several other successful experiments have also been reported. One of the strongest of these is an experiment looking for information relating to the 70 nations described in the Torah as being the descendants of Noah and his sons. These experiments can be viewed at: www.torahcodes.co.il/whatsnew.htm.

C) The Challenge

In the eyes of the critics, the central problem in the Rabbi's experiment is the claim that the researchers could have cheated using the "wiggle room" available within the rules established by Professor Havlin. In addition to unequivocal refutations of their arguments, **the researchers openly proposed a public challenge to the critics well over one year ago:** to come to an agreement with us on the appointment of a new independent expert in Rabbinic bibliographical data, and to have him construct his own list of appellations using the original guidelines.

We are still waiting for their response to the challenge.

Myth #6:

The Torah texts we possess today are substantially corrupt compared to original texts.

Fact:

The simple fact is that the researchers ran their experiment on the *Textus Receptus*, by far the most widely used text in circulation in Jewish communities around the world. While there may be slight variations in other extant versions of Torah texts, the differences are much too negligible to have a serious detrimental effect on the results.[8]

In addition, a simple logical argument shows that this criticism is meaningless. There is a difference of opinion among scholars as to how much the text of the original Torah has been corrupted. Some say it has been corrupted by many errors, while others say that no more than a single letter is in question. Thus, one can reason as follows: (1) There is very strong statistical evidence that the codes are real; (2) If there are few errors in the Torah, the statistical evidence for codes will still be there, albeit not as strong had there been no errors at all; (3) if there are many errors in the Torah, the statistical evidence of codes would vanish completely. We therefore conclude that there are at most few errors in the Torah, as some experts claim. The critics' position that there <u>must</u> be many errors is thus logically untenable.

Section A: Some of the Jewish Sources for Codes

אֵ The great teacher of the Ramban, Rabbi Eliezer (Rokeach), in the introduction to his commentary on the Torah, describes "73 ways to understand and interpret the letters of the Torah." Number 54 is called "the way of skipping."

אֵ An example of an ELS code is explicitly mentioned in a commentary on the Torah written by Rabbi Bachya in 1291 (chapter 1, verse 2).

אֵ The renowned Rabbi Moshe Cordovero, head of the Rabbinical Court of Tzfat, wrote a book called *Pardes Rimonim* in 1549. On page 68, he writes that the secrets of the Torah are revealed in its letters through many means, including "skipping of letters".

אֵ In 1957, the students of Rabbi Michoel Ber Weissmandl published a book called Torat Chemed that contains many examples of letter skipping patterns found by their teacher.

Section B: Rabbinic Endorsements

There are letters available to the public by some of today's leading Rabbis. They deal with:

a. Confirmation that there is an accepted Jewish tradition that there are ELS codes in the Torah,
b. the reliability of the researchers and the accuracy of their data,
c. the encouragement to research and publicize the findings of Torah codes.

Letters are available in the original Hebrew, as well as translations, from: Rabbi Shlomo Fisher (his own letter, plus one attesting to the endorsement of the late Rabbi Shlomo Zalman Auerbach ztz'l), Rabbi Shmuel Kamenetsky, Rabbi Shmuel Auerbach, Rabbi Shmuel Deutsch, Rabbi Shlomo Wolbe ztz'l, and Rabbi Matisyahu Solomon.

It is worthy to note as well, that *not one* rabbinic authority has endorsed the claims of the critics.

Following is a letter of approbation from the renowned Rabbi Shlomo Wolbe *ztz'l*.

2 Marcheshvan 5759

It is known that a way exists to discover hints and matters from the Torah by reading letters at equidistant intervals. This method is found in the commentary of Rabeinu Bechai on the Torah and the works of Rav Moshe Cordovero. More recently, the tzaddik, Rav Weissmandel, revealed wondrous things with this method. To my surprise, I have heard that opponents to this method have arisen claiming that various deceptions were performed by those who are involved in this method today. It is astonishing to me that they were not intimidated to state their claims after the Gaon Rav Shlomo Zalman Auerbach gave his clear agreement to the method of equidistant intervals, and after Rav Auerbach's son, the Gaon Rav Shmuel, censured them. I am uncertain of these opponent's intentions. Are they troubled that at seminars to make people religious, that these astonishing matters are sometimes taught and their effect on the listeners is profound? Is this what is bothering them? Whatever the reason of those who oppose this method, it is certainly not a dispute for the sake of heaven, and we must strengthen those who are engaged in this method, for it is a totally honest endeavor. May they be encouraged and see blessed results to their deeds, and may they continue to increase the honor of our holy Torah and its influence on all who seek the Almighty's closeness. May the Almighty help those who engage for the sake of heaven in this honest discipline of studying equidistant intervals,

Shlomo Wolbe

Section C: What is an ELS code?

To fully understand the method of finding and evaluating the codes, one must read the full technical description given in the paper in Statistical Science.(Vol. 9 , issue 3. June 1994). However, the following simplified explanation will give the reader a rough impression of the nature of the research. The claim made by the researchers is roughly as follows:

1. ELSs (Equidistant Letter Sequences) are words spelled out in a text by skipping an equal number of letters.

2. Any word may appear several times at different skip intervals in the same text- i.e. the word "hammer" may appear in a text every 4th letter at a certain point, somewhere else every 29th letter,

somewhere else every 245th letter, etc. One of these occurrences will be the "minimal" ELS. (in this example, the ELS of 4).[9]

3. We observe that in the Hebrew text of Genesis, the minimal ELSs of related words (i.e. "hammer" and "anvil") appear encoded in close proximity to each other.

4. We perform objective experiments on large sets of pairs of words and demonstrate that this effect (called "the proximity of related ELSs") occurs much more often than would be statistically expected.

Section D: The debate over spellings of names

When the critics manipulated their list of names to make it succeed in War and Peace, they consistently violated basic rules of spelling and grammar. At times, they went even beyond, and had difficulty even just looking up names. Here we will cite only one flagrant example:

They attempted to prove that Rabbi Moshe Zacuta's name does not appear in the form "Zacuta" (זכותא) (as was used in the original experiment), but only as "Zacut" (זכות). To this end they cite the title page of his biography, where the name "Zacut" indeed appears. Had they turned one more page they would have seen that in the Polish title the name appears as "Zacuta", and in the German as "Zakuto." In the text itself the name זכותא appears at the top of every page!

For a detailed analysis, see the full refutation of the critics' data at www.torahcodes.co.il

---

1 See the article ELSs in the Book of Genesis, printed in Statistical Science, June 1994. The research was conducted by Doron Witztum, along with Professor Eliyahu Rips, a world-renowned mathematician.

2 At one point, in lieu of any of their arguments being accepted for publication, the critics went so far as to gather a *petition* of scientists who are opposed to the research being carried out. When was the last time a scientific issue was decided by petition?

3 The original published statistic was 16/1,000,000, or p=.000016. The experiment was later re-run on a more expansive set of control tests and achieved the result of 59/100,000,000. After taking into account possible optimizations, the results changed to 19/100,000,000!

4 An expert in linguistics, Yaakov Orbach ob"m, was also consulted regarding the proper way of referring to Hebrew dates.

5 Note too, that independent Rabbinic authorities, in a public letter, stated that "we checked the rules according to which Professor Havlin formulated his list of names and titles of Torah leaders, and we found that it was com-

mensurate with both professional standards and common sense.. The list is in keeping with the principles. We found that all the claims concerning the opponents' individual claims concerning deviation from the principles to be false".

6 To quote Harold Gans: "It is important to note that the list of places of birth and death were obtained using a precise and detailed linguistic protocol to ensure accurate data and accurate spelling. In spite of the fact that this experiment directly corroborates [the Witztum-Rips] Famous Rabbis experiment, and has been public knowledge for over eight years, no one has ever succeeded in producing a counterfeit of this experiment. The strict use of a precise protocol effectively blocks any attempt to cheat."

7 Professor Rips ran a similar experiment, focusing only on the names of Jacob's twelve sons, and also using other variant sources for the dates of death. He too achieved significant results. His experiment is available at www.ma.huji.ac.il/~rips

8 The one other well-accepted text of the Torah is the standard one used by Yemenite communities, in which there are 8 variations over the 304,805-letter text of the Torah. When tests were run on the Yemenite version of Genesis, the results remained significant.

9 Other ELSs that are not the minimum, but are minimal over large areas of the text are also considered, but their effect is pro-rated in kind.

Appendix

The Accuracy of Our Written Torah

By Rabbi Dovid Lichtman

Our Torah scroll is perhaps our most revered physical possession today. The honor and respect with which we handle our Torah in synagogue results from our knowledge that it contains the words of Hashem as dictated to Moshe over 3300 years ago. Meticulous care has been taken to insure the proper transmission of the Torah. There are many factors, which collectively contribute to the wholeness of the Torah, but perhaps the single most important factor is the orthography, or proper spelling of each word. In fact, the orthography of the Torah is considered so important that the scribe is instructed to "be careful with your task, for it is sacred work; if you add or subtract even a single letter, [it is as if] you have destroyed the entire world!" (Eruvin 13a). The Rambam writes (Hil. Sefer Torah 7:11) that if one letter is added to or missing from a Torah, it is invalidated and is not conferred the sanctity of a Torah scroll. Special mechanisms were established by the Sages to ensure its accurate transmission through the generations (see, for example, Megilah 18b; YD #274). (From the wording of the Rambam, it appears that this is true even if the wanton letter does not affect the meaning of the word. This is also the ruling of the Tikunei ha'Zohar (#25), Ramban end of Introduction to the Torah, Magen Avraham and Vilna Gaon OC 143:4, Sha'agat Aryeh (#36), Chatam Sofer (OC #52), in contrast to Minchat Chinuch's ruling (#613) that a missing or additional letter does not invalidate a Torah scroll unless it affects either a word's pronunciation or its literal or exegetical meaning.) Originally, the Torah was so well preserved that every letter was counted (Kiddushin 30a), which is why the early scribes were given the title "Soferim" ("Counters/Scribes"). Thousands of traditions were handed down specifying orthographic details. One of the more well-known is that the letter 'Vav' of the word 'Gachon' Parasha Vayikra (11:42) is the middle letter of the Torah (Kiddushin, ibid. -- refer to Rabbi Kornfeld's "Torah from the Internet" p. 122 for an in-depth discussion of this and similar traditions.)

Indeed, the text of today's Torah scrolls the world over are uniform, with very few exceptions. As we will demonstrate, the Mesorah (transmitted tradition) of our text was well tended to; its margin of error appears to be less than .00004, and to involve only insignificant letters at that. However, upon investigation it is evident that there existed many variants among older Torah scrolls. This prompts us to ask a number of questions: (a) First, one must ask how it came to be that there existed such diverse texts. Did they derive from individual copyists' errors, or were there differing Mesorot? (b) Second, one must ask how we came to accept at present one text as "correct" from among the many that once existed. (c) Third, can we have any degree of certainty that the present day unified text is the accurate text of the Torah as transmitted to and transcribed by Moshe? In this essay, we will attempt to address these questions.

II

Originally, it was easy to attend to the Mesorah of the Torah text. A Torah scroll written in Moshe's own hand was kept in or near the Holy Ark in the Holy of Holies (Bava Batra 14a). This text, which apparently was accessible to the Kohanim (Rashi Bava Batra 14b s.v. Sefer; see also Tosefot, Bava Batra 14a s.v. Shelo), undoubtedly served as the proof text for all other texts. The scroll which each Jewish king was required to write and bear at all times was likewise copied from this scroll (Rambam, Hil. Sefer Torah 7:2, based on Yerushalmi Sanhedrin 2:6). The kingly scrolls, in turn, served as proof texts after their owner's death.

The destruction of the first Beit ha'Mikdash most likely brought with it the destruction of these proof texts. Ezra the Scribe, who led the people back to Eretz Yisrael and began to rebuild the Beit ha'Mikdash, set to reestablishing a proof text. At this point, a defining event occurred. According to the Talmud Yerushalmi (Ta'anit 4:2), three ancient scrolls were found in the Temple confines, which had slightly variant texts. (Although the Yerushalmi does not specify when this occurred, other sources relate that it happened in the days of Ezra and according to some versions, it was Ezra himself who found the scrolls -- see Torah Sheleimah, Shemot 24 note 29.) The Yerushalmi then relates that the correct version of the Torah was determined by virtue of a majority of 2 against 1.

Throughout the period of the Second Beit ha'Mikdash, a scroll referred to as 'Sefer Ezra' or 'Sefer Ha'azarah' (Moed Katan 18b) served as the standard for all others. Sefer Ha'azarah was either the very scroll that was written by Ezra the Scribe or one that was copied from it (Rashi, ibid.). Professional Soferim were employed at the Beit ha'Mikdash to correct private scrolls based on this scroll (Ketuvot 106a; Shekalim 10b). These highly accurate scrolls and their copies remained the standard until well after the destruction of the second Beit ha'Mikdash. The Talmud in Kiddushim (30a) establishes that the accurate counting of the letters of the Torah was preserved at least until Tanaitic times (2nd century CE).

III

A century or so later, in the times of the Amora'im, Rav Yosef commented that this accuracy was already somewhat diluted. Such a lack of accuracy can only have been made apparent by the existence of divergent texts. The Gemara makes it clear that even this dilution of accuracy was only with regard to Malei and Chaser. (Malei and Chaser refer to unpronounced letters, such as 'Vav' and 'Yud,' which lend added accent to vowels. Their presence or absence does not affect the meaning of a word). Nor does the Gemara state in how many instances doubts arose regarding orthography. It is possible that these uncertainties were limited to a very few instances. In fact, nowhere in the Talmud or Midrashic sources is there recorded a dispute over the orthography of a specific Malei or Chaser, either before or after the time of Rav Yosef. (It should be pointed out that according to some, Rav Yosef was merely stating that *he* could not determine the exact number of letters in the Torah, since he himself was blind and could not count them by heart and he was not willing to rely on another person's count -- see Rav Reuvain Margulies in "HaMikra V'HaMesorah," #4).

Due to the dispersal of the Jewish people and the lack of a central supervising authority, variations in scrolls continued. Authorities in Israel and Bavel, independently, undertook to produce one highly accurate text. These authorities, called the Masorites, thrived and produced such works between the 8th and 10th centuries. Their methodology, which was based on the system described by the Yerushalmi Ta'anit (above, section II), may be called the "eclectic process," or majority rule. Simply stated, this process involves surveying a great variety of Torah scrolls whereby each letter of the text is compared and contrasted. The correct orthography is determined based on the majority of texts, and hence errors are weeded out. For example, if in a survey of 200 Sifrei Torah, 198 were found to have in one particular place a spelling of "honour" and 2 were found to have the spelling as `honor', it may be assumed that the former is the correct orthography, while the latter were introduced by careless scribes. (Of course, the eclectic process can only be employed using older texts of good standing to some degree. This is evident from the fact that only the three scrolls found in the Temple confines were considered for the process, in the time of Ezra. After all, certainly hundreds of scrolls were in existence at the time.)

The crowning jewel of the master texts produced in this manner was the one produced in Teveryah by Aharon ben Moshe ben Asher (known simply as "Ben Asher") of the late 10th century. The Rambam extols his text as being extremely accurate and it was adopted by the Rambam and many others as the standard (Rambam, Hil. Sefer Torah, beginning of 8:4). In the Rambam's time, this Torah was known to be in Alexandria, Egypt. (Traditionally, the "Keter Aram Tzova," or Aleppo Codex, presently in Yerushalayim, is purported to be the Ben Asher manuscript. Unfortunately, only the Nevi'im and Ketuvim sections of this manuscript remain intact, as virtually the entire Torah section of the manuscript was lost to fire a few decades ago.)

Today, the Teimani (Yemenite) Torah scrolls are very likely exact copies of this text. It is well known that the Yemenite Jews adhered firmly to the Rambam's rulings in every matter of Halachah. The limited size and dispersion of their community throughout the generations made it much easier for them to preserve their Mesorah. Indeed, there is no variance among Teimani scrolls today.

Despite the Rambam's efforts to ensure the perpetuation of one standardized text, divergent scrolls began to propagate once again. A contemporary of the Ramban, the RaMaH (Rav Meir Halevi Abulafia -- early 13th century), undertook to reestablish a text of exceptional accuracy. The RaMaH again used the eclectic process, surveying hundreds of old and reputable scrolls. (RaMaH did not have the Ben Asher manuscript at his disposal.) The resultant text was published in his work "Mesores Seyag la'Torah." Given the great effort that RaMaH invested in this project and his standing as a leading Halachic authority, his work became the definitive standard until today, certainly with regard to orthography (see Ohr Torah, Minchat Shai and Keset ha'Sofer).

We have thus answered the first two of our questions: (a) Since a standard, approved Mesorah for the Torah text existed throughout much of our history, in all probability the variant texts of early Torahs may be attributed to sloppy copyists, who did not carefully compare their work with the Masoretic proof-text of the times, or were not able to do so. (b) The manner in which the mistaken texts were weeded out from the correct ones was the eclectic process of the Yerushalmi in Ta'anit, which has been employed regularly since the time of Chazal in order to ensure proper transmission of the Torah.

IV

(c) However, we have not yet addressed our third question: Can it be scientifically demonstrated that our text is indeed the correct one (i.e., that the eclectic process worked)? Halachically, we are secure in our reliance on the eclectic process (Teshuvot Ginat Veradim 1:2:6). This does not mean, though, that our Mesorah is 100% in agreement with the original text that was handed to us by Moshe. It only means that we are doing our best and are following the dictates of Halachah in determining how to write our Torahs. In fact, many authorities write that our texts may very well not match up with the true Mosaic text (authorities in OC 143:4, Sha'agat Aryeh. Chatam Sofer and Minchat Chinuch cited at the beginning of section I, see Hagaon Rav Moshe Sternbuch in "Mitzvat ha'Yom," pp. 32-43, who discusses the Halachic aspects of this statement in detail.). But does that mean that our texts may be "wildly inaccurate", or that "one or two" discrepancies may exist? Or, returning to our first question, can it be proven that enough attention was given to preserving the Mesorah and that copyists' errors were usually nipped in the bud before assuming the part of "Mesorah?" Or did too long a time pass between Masoretic overhauls, and many errors became independent Mesorahs over the years? (This theoretical question has been brought to the forefront in recent years by the great Torah Codes debate.) Rav Mordechai Breuer of Yerushalayim has conducted an exercise regarding this very question, with fascinating results.

In his work, "The Aleppo Codex and the Accepted Text of the Torah", Rav Breuer describes his years of meticulous research and discusses his conclusions in attempting to demonstrate the scientific usefulness of the eclectic process. In fact, Rav Breuer's purpose was to demonstrate that a single Mesorah already existed in the years prior to the RaMaH, even though the RaMaH did not have such a Mesorah at his disposal. (Many academicians flatly reject the existence of such a single Mesorah.) Rav Breuer began by selecting four texts of ancient origin to compare and contrast in his study. Each of these texts predates the RaMaH. The texts were all of the type written by the Tiberian Masorites (as opposed to the Babylonian Masorites) yet clearly differed from each other in certain significant formatting areas, indicating that they were not copied from an immediate common source. In addition, he included the text of the Mikra'ot Gedolot of Yaakov ben Chaim, printed in Venice, 1525. (It should be noted that the orthography of these 5 texts differed widely from one another, in one case by more than 200 letters from the others.) Using the eclectic process, he suggested that if a broad majority of 4 out of 5 texts (and not just 3 of the 5) agreed with each other, it could be assumed that the fifth, inconsistent text was a copyist's error. His results were startling. There are 304,805 letters in the Torah. All five texts were in **total** agreement in all but about 220 letters. Of these, all but **20** were resolved by a majority of at least 4 texts against 1! Of the 20 remaining conflicts, Rav Breuer was able to clarify all but **6** by applying another Masorite method, that of carefully studying thousands of early Masoretic notes (a broader topic similar in style to the eclectic process). It was apparent that nearly all of the inconsistencies between the Torahs were caused by copyists errors, and not by Masoretic uncertainties.

Next, the resultant 'eclectic' text was compared with the RaMaH's text (i.e., our present text). It was found that the RaMaH differed in but **6** places from the eclectic. That is, the margin of uncertainty of our Torah scrolls is probably not more than 12 (out of 304,805!) letters -- the 6 indeterminate ones, plus the six in which the RaMaH's text differed from Rav Breuer's eclectic! When he compared the results of his experiment with the Teimani text (which, as we mentioned, is probably identical to that of Ben Asher), the results were even more startling. The texts were in perfect agreement! Equally amazing is that **all** the above-mentioned differences involve Vavs and Yuds, which do not affect the meaning of the word at all. (As for the remaining six uncertainties in Rav Breuer's eclectic survey, in three of the instances the RaMaH and Teimani texts agreed with the 3-against-2-majority text. In the other three cases, the RaMaH and Teimani texts were themselves split over the same variant spellings, as were the pre-RaMaH texts. In total, that means that the Teimani text, which is identical to the eclectic text, differs from the RaMaH's text in but **9** letters -- see endnotes for details.)

In conclusion, the transmission of our Torah text has been well tended to and well preserved. The methods of Chazal have proudly withstood the tests of time. Such demonstrations of the strength of our Mesorah are indeed a Kiddush Hashem.

The author welcomes your comments on the above article. Send comments to DLichtman@aish.com

ENDNOTES:

Torah variants of Rav Breuer's results, as compared to our (=RaMaH's) Torahs, in order of appearance (E=eclectic; T=Teimani): (1) Bereishit 4:13 "Mineso" (E&T w/o Vav); (2) Bereishit 7:11 "Ma'ayanos (E&T w/o Vav); (3) Bereishit 9:29 "Vayehi" (E&T Vayiheyu); (4) Bereishit 46:13 "v'Shimron" (E with Vav); (5) Shemot 14:22 "Chomah" (E w/o Vav); (6) Shemot 25:31 "Te'aseh"

(E&T w/o Yud); (7) Shemot 28:26 "ha'Efod" (E&T w/o Vav); (8) Bamidbar 1:17 "b'Shemot" (T w/o Vav); (9) Bamidbar 10:10 "Chodsheichem" (T with Yud); (10) Bamidbar 22:5 "Be'or" (T w/o Vav); (11) Bamidbar 33:52 "Bamo-tam" (E w/o Vav); (12) Devarim 23:2 "Daka" (E&T with Alef instead of Heh. Lubavitch Chassidic texts are in agreement with T in this matter).

Endnotes

Introduction

1 http://www.physlink.com/Education/askExperts/ae535.cfm

2 Deuteronomy 4:39

3 Rabbi Moshe Chaim Luzzatto, *The Way of God*, Section 1:1

How Did That Happen?

4 Mark Twain, from the article "Concerning the Jews" first printed in Harpers (1899). Reprinted in *The Complete Works of Mark Twain*, Doubleday, 1963, page 249

5 Leo Tolstoy, from the periodical "Jewish World" published in London, 1908

6 John Adams, from a letter to F.A. Van der Kemp, 1808, the Pennsylvania Historical Society

7 See *The Living Torah*, by Aryeh Kaplan, Mozniam Publishing Corporation, 1981

8 See the Babylonian Talmud, Megilah 6A and 6B for the Jewish take on the history of this translation

9 For an excellent summary of pre-State Israel see *Israel: A History*, Martin Glibert, Harper Perennial, 2008, Chapters 1-9

10 See *From Time Immemorial: The Origins of the Arab-Jewish Conflict Over Palestine*, Joan Peters, Harper & Row 1984, *Chapter 3: The Arab Jew*, Pages 33-71

11 *Next to the Angel of Death: How I Hung and Cremated Eichmann*, Yitzhak Nachshoni and Asher Medina, *Shofar News*, April 28, 2004. Eichmann's executioner was also one of his guards, Shalom Nagar, a Yemenite Jew.

http://www.historama.com/online-resources/articles/israel/shalom_
nagar_eichmanns_hangman.html

12 Genesis 17:7

13 "As a result of the relentless persecutions and forced expulsions, most Jews
are but recent new-comers to their respective lands of residence. 90% of
the Jewish people have lived in their new homes for no more than 100
years. The majority of the large Jewish settlements date back no more than
50 or 60 years! 75% of Jewry has thus been displaced in three lands (Israel,
America, and Russia) while the remaining 25% are dispersed throughout
over 100 lands on all five continents." Quoted from Leschzinsky, *The Jewish
Dispersion*, page 9 and translated from Hebrew – taken from an early edition
of the Discovery Sourcebook.

14 http://www.whitehouse.gov/about/presidents/DwightDEisenhower

15 Leviticus 26:33

16 I found many different studies, this article looks at a few: http://www.
simpletoremember.com/vitals/world-jewish-population.htm

17 http://www.jewishvirtuallibrary.org/jsource/Judaism/fsuemig.html

18 Deuteronomy 4:27

19 *The Way to Victory of the Germanic Spirit over the Jewish Spirit*

20 Quoted from Professor Michael Curtis of Rutgers University

21 Check out the *Protocols of the Elders of Zion* – the mother of all conspiracy
theories

22 I found this list online here: http://www.biblebelievers.org.au/expelled.htm
- judging from the wording, they probably took it from the same place as the
Discovery Sourcebook (where I first saw it). The site links to this: http://
www.sunray22b.net/expulsions.htm - it is a list of sources for most of the
places on the list.

23 *The New York Times* called General Orders No. 11 issued by Major General
U.S. Grant on December 17, 1862 "one of the deepest sensations of the
war." Grant's order read:

> The Jews, as a class violating every regulation of trade established
> by the Treasury Department and also department orders, are here-
> by expelled from the department within twenty-four hours from
> the receipt of this order.
>
> Post commanders will see to it that all of this class of people be
> furnished passes and required to leave, and any one returning af-
> ter such notification will be arrested and held in confinement until
> an opportunity occurs of sending them out as prisoners, unless
> furnished with permit from headquarters. No passes will be given
> these people to visit headquarters for the purpose of making per-
> sonal application of trade permits.

Taken from http://www.jewishvirtuallibrary.org/jsource/loc/abe2.html quoting Abraham J. Karp, *From the Ends of the Earth: Judaic Treasures of the Library of Congress*, (DC: Library of Congress, 1991).

24 *Ending College Admission Quotas Against Asian-Americans*, Dan C. Heldman, June 30, 1989, http://www.heritage.org/research/education/em240.cfm

25 Found reference to this article online: "New Jewish Unit Plans University," *The New York Times*, August 20, 1946, p. 10.

26 *Outliers: The Story of Success*, Malcolm Gladwell, Little Brown and Company, 2008, *Chapter 5: Three Lessons from Joe Flom*

27 Leviticus 26:36

28 See *Ancient Rome*, Robert Payne, American Heritage Inc. 1966 for an excellent overview of Roman History. I took these facts from there.

29 Malise Ruthven, *Islam: A Very Short Introduction*, Oxford University Press, 1997. Pages 35-39.

30 See *From Time Immemorial: The Origins of the Arab-Jewish Conflict Over Palestine*, Joan Peters, Harper & Row 1984, *Chapter 3: The Arab Jew*, Pages 33-71

31 http://www.jewishvirtuallibrary.org/jsource/Judaism/nobels.html

32 Ernest van den Haag, *The Jewish Mystique*, Stein & Day Pub (April 1977), first published in 1968

33 Isaiah 42:6

34 For an excellent account of this entire period, see *The Jewish War* by Josephus. I have the Penguin Classics Edition translated by G.A. Williamson in 1959 and revised by E. Mary Smallwood in 1970

35 *Ancient Rome*, Robert Payne, American Heritage Inc. 1966 for an excellent overview of Roman History, page 259

36 See *Israel: A History*, Martin Glibert, Harper Perennial, 2008

37 The Land of Israel, Palestine, Judea, and Israel are interchangeable names for the same place.

38 http://www.jewishvirtuallibrary.org/jsource/vie/Caesarea.html

39 See Bernard Lewis *The Middle East: A Brief History of the Last 2,000 Years* (1995 Touchstone/Simon & Schuster)

40 *From Time Immemorial: The Origins of the Arab-Jewish Conflict Over Palestine*, Joan Peters, Harper & Row 1984, Pages 167-168: "By the end of the nineteenth century the political power was in the hands of those Muslim families 'with names like al-Husayni, al-Khalidi, and al-Nashashibi.' The 'parasitic landlord class' had acquired, through the *fellahins'* ruinous indebtedness, huge landholdings, which the landlords seldom if ever visited, and almost never farmed."

41 Nachmonides (Rabbi Moshe ben Nachman), *Epistle to his Son*, 1260

42 Mark Twain, *The Innocents Abroad or The New Pilgrim's Progress*, Volume II, Harper and Brothers, NY, 1922, Pages 216-359

43 See *Crash Course in Jewish History: from Abraham to Modern Israel*, Ken Spiro, Published by aish.com and Targum Press, 2010

44 Also see *Start-Up Nation: The Story of Israel's Economic Miracle*, Dan Senor and Saul Singer, Twelve, 2009, Pages 15-17 (Actually, amazing stats are scattered throughout the book)

45 Leviticus 26:32-33

46 Deuteronomy 30:3-5

47 *Israel: A History*, Martin Gilbert, Harper Perennial, 2008, page 15: Herzl wrote: "At Basle I founded the Jewish State. If I said this out loud today, I would be answered by universal laughter. Perhaps in five years, and certainly in fifty, everyone will know it."

You Do the Math

48 Sifra Ditzniuta, Chapter 5

49 Pardes Rimonim, 68A

50 Rabbi Cordovero was not the first person to discuss skipping letters. Also see the Rokeach (Rabbi Eleazar ben Judah ben Kalonymus of Worms, 1176 – 1238) in the introduction to his commentary on the Torah. He lists 73 ways to understand and interpret the letters of the Torah. Number 54 is "the way of skipping." Also see the Rabbainu Bachya's commentary on the Torah (written in 1291), chapter 1, verse 2. You can read a full description about Rabbainu Bachya's code and its meaning here: http://www.torahcode.net/first_els/first_els.shtml

51 He was also known as Michael Ber Weissmandl

52 Many people ask, "What is the significance of fifty?" The best answer is, I don't know. Any interval is interesting. Fifty is a significant number in the Torah – fifty days between the Exodus and the experience at Mt. Sinai, fifty years in the Jubilee cycle – but I don't know for sure.

53 http://torahcode.us/people/rips.shtml

54 The complete early history of codes research is here: http://torahcode.us/torah_codes/code_history/code_history1.shtml - Rabbi Shmuel Yaniv was the first person to introduce Rips to Rabbi Weissmandl's findings. Yaniv wrote a multi volume work called Hidden Things in the Torah. Avraham Oren showed Rips more advanced searches that led to the "Aaron Code" – his first big find. Read all the details at the link above.

55 Some of Rips's early findings were published in 1988 in the Journal of the Royal Statistical Society, Series A, Volume 151, p165

56 http://torahcode.us/people/witztum.shtml

57 *Lechah Dodi* is a liturgical poem read every Friday night in synagogue. Rabbi Shlomo HaLevi Alkabetz wrote it. His name, Shlomo HaLevi, is hidden in the first letter of the first eight stanzas.

58 The *Mishna Torah* by Maimonides and the *Path of the Just* by Rabbi Moshe Chaim Luzzatto are two great examples.

59 See *The Living Torah*, by Aryeh Kaplan, Mozniam Publishing Corporation, 1981

60 See the Babylonian Talmud, Megilah 6A and 6B for the Jewish take on the history of this translation

61 Technically, the final form of Mem – ם – is used here, but the letters are interchangeable

62 They actually ran many tests, but for the sake of simplicity I am limiting the number of examples

63 At the time, the Book of Genesis was the only book of the Torah that had a reliable version that existed in a computable form.

64 If you look carefully at the example, it says "HaChanukah" – The Chanukah. Chanukah is Hebrew for dedication. The miracle of Chanukah happened during the rededication of the Temple. The Chanukah was the dedication.

65 Technically speaking, a code is something you can scientifically verify (as is proven by the experiments discussed below). I am using the term here loosely to refer to any equidistant skip found anywhere – whether it is scientific or not.

66 http://www.diabetes.org/diabetes-basics/type-2/

67 http://www.med.uni-giessen.de/itr/history/inshist.html

68 I took part of the story of modern codes research and subsequent publication in Statistical Science from transcripts of the "Bible Codes" class that is a part of the Discovery Seminar. The transcripts are not publically available, however, much of the information can be found here: http://torahsearch.com/page.cfm/3126. In reality, the order of events may be different than presented here and in the Discovery transcripts. According to this site - http://torahcode.us/torah_codes/code_history/code_history1.shtml - the Great Rabbis Experiment was run first and then shown to Statistical Science - not as part of a negotiation as presented here. Regardless, the experiment that was actually published was the second experiment that involved Diaconis as discussed below.

69 The order of events, as presented here, is also from transcripts of the "Bible Codes" class from the Discovery Seminar. It has been brought to my attention that the actual sequence of events is different. An accurate version is posted on Doron Witztum's website here: http://www.torahcode.co.il/home_eng.htm

I decided not to change the narrative in this edition because:

a. This narrative does a good job (and I think the more important job) of explaining the concept of hidden failures.

b. This narrative doesn't affect the results or contradict the ultimate conclusions published in Statistical Science.

70 The rabbi's names were listed in two different ways: a) as a name, i.e. the way he would be called up to the Torah (and how he was probably referred to in his lifetime), and b) as an appellation, i.e. the way he is commonly referred to after his death. For example, Maimonides's name would be Rabbi Moshe ben Maimon and his appellation would be RAMBAM.

71 If you want to read about the Torah codes, the experiments, the math, the definition of terms, and the results in all their gory detail, check out A Primer on the Torah Codes Controversy for Laymen by Harold J. Gans. You can download it as a PDF here: http://www.torahcode.net/primer-final-1.pdf

72 Using this method – choosing only rabbis with three or more columns written about them – was an objective way to formulate the data set. It meant that the list wasn't biased or subjective. It also meant that the list was a *priori*, i.e. stated in advance. (As opposed to a *posteriori* or stated after the fact.)

73 The experiment only "looked" successful because at the time they did not know how to measure the probability (and that meant they could not determine if the names and dates were in close mathematical proximity). Persi Diaconis solved the problem in his review of the experiment. He suggested using a randomization process (not a formula) and described how to do it efficiently.

74 See note 69 – this exchange with Statistical Science may be fictitious.

75 http://stat.stanford.edu/~cgates/PERSI/cv.html

76 http://news-service.stanford.edu/news/2004/june9/diaconis-69.html

77 See note 72

78 The Samaritan Torah is very similar to the Masoretic text (some say as much as 98% similar). They differ in a number of ways that are theologically significant. You can read more about the differences here: http://web.meson.org/religion/torahcompare.php

79 The version of War and Peace they used was truncated to the first 78,064 letters (the same length as the Book of Genesis).

80 The technical details of the agreement between Professors Diaconis and Aumann involved the number of random permutations and the requisite level of significance. Rips and Witztum were not involved in the negotiation and were joined by a third scientist, Yoav Rosenberg.

Rips, Witztum, and Rosenberg wrote the paper for publication – before running the experiment – leaving out the results (which didn't yet exist). They sent the paper to Diaconis and a few other statisticians.

Diaconis, along with the other statisticians, approved the experiment as it was described in the paper. They each independently stipulated the level of significance that should be required.

The experiment was run and the results were significant: $p = 0.000016$, well beyond the proposed cutoffs. The results were incorporated into the paper.

Go here to read more of what I paraphrased above: http://torahsearch.com/page.cfm/3206

81 It is important to note that this was not a second requirement for publication. It is merely another way of describing the results.

82 You can look it up – *Statistical Science: a review journal of the institute of mathematical statistics*, Volume 9, Number 3, August 1994. *Equidistant Letter Sequences in the Book of Genesis* by D. Witztum, E. Rips, and Y. Rosenberg, pages 429-438.

83 *Statistical Science: a review journal of the institute of mathematical statistics*, Volume 14, Number 2 (1999), *Solving the Bible Code Puzzle*, by Brendan McKay, Dror Bar-Natan, Maya Bar-Hillel, and Gil Kalai, pages 150-173.

84 According to Moshe Zeldman – one of the main codes teachers for the Discovery Seminar – Randy Ingermanson found the error in the original formula. Ingermanson has an excellent website about the bible codes and also wrote the book, Who Wrote the Bible Code? Go here to see more: http://www.ingermanson.com/codes/index.php. The more important point is that although the critics had problems with some of the names on the list, their primary concern was that Rips and Witztum manipulated their data to achieve desirable results (as I noted in the text).

85 This number is from the transcript of the "Bible Codes" class from the Discovery seminar. According to Moshe Zeldman, it is from internal correspondence between Witztum/Rips/Rosenberg and some of those involved in trying to refute the experiment. Moshe Zeldman confirmed this number as well as the results from the "Talmud" and "Cities of Joshua" experiments mentioned later. I was not able to find these experiments on the pro-codes websites, though they are available in Israel (and much of the work was done in the early 90's, before it was common practice to post on the Internet. But note, there is no shortage of scientifically verifiable codes research online. This site is a good start: http://torahcode.org/). According to Harold Gans, the more important refutation to the critics is the peer-reviewed papers from the 18th International Conference on Pattern Recognition (2006). See note 91

86 A detailed response to frequently asked questions and misconceptions about the Torah codes is posted here: http://torahsearch.com/page.cfm/3212 and reprinted in the appendix

87 See note 70 - or more accurately, the critics claimed that they doctored their choice of appellations

88 The critics proved that it is possible to fudge the results. They did not prove that Rips and Witztum fudged their results.

89 He used the same spellings and appellations (see note 70 above)

90 Most of the articles online attacking the bible codes fall into one of two groups. The first group attacks the book The Bible Code by Michael Drosnin. The second group attacks the serious scientific research noted here.

91 You can download preprints for all seven papers here: http://www.torah-codes.net/paper7.html

92 http://www.comp.hkbu.edu.hk/~icpr06/

93 These papers were peer-reviewed by the 18th International Conference on Pattern Recognition and were published in the proceedings of that conference. Because of the unusual nature of the papers, between four and six reviewers were assigned to each.

94 According to Harold Gans, the combined odds against both the Gans and original Rips/Witztum experiments happening by chance are 1:638,569,604.

The Pig's Foot

95 Leviticus 11:4-8

96 Chulin 59a: The Academy of Rebbe Yishmael taught: The Torah states, "The camel shall be unclean to you although *it* chews its cud." The Ruler of the Universe knows that only the camel chews its cud but remains unclean. Therefore, the verse specifies "it."

97 http://www.reshafim.org.il/ad/egypt/timelines/topics/zoos.htm - quoting from numerous sources

98 Chulin 60b

99 The Torah clearly states that the *shafan* and *arneves* are cud-chewing animals. According to Torah sources, cud-chewing is distinguished by five criteria:

- א The animal regurgitates nearly all its food
- א The food is regurgitated as a bolus (soft ball)
- א The animal chews this bolus
- א The animal chews the bolus using a lateral motion
- א This process is done for imperative nutritional purposes

A number of translators have suggested translations for *shafan* and *arneves*; however, none of their suggestions fit these five criteria. Some have suggested that caecotrophy (when an animal re-ingests soft pellets of semi-digested matter taken directly from the anus) could be considered cud chewing. Based on the criteria listed above, caecotrophy clearly doesn't fit the bill. Based on these factors, it is best to consider the *shafan* and *arneves* likely extinct.

See MICHAEL ALLABY. "caecotrophy." A Dictionary of Zoology. 1999. Encyclopedia.com. 8 Mar. 2010 <http://www.encyclopedia.com> for a definition of caecotrophy

The Jewish Experience at Mount Sinai

100 For a great overview of Roman History see Robert Payne, *Ancient Rome* (1966 American Heritage Inc/iBooks)

101 Tom Holland *Rubicon: The Last Years of the Roman Republic* (2003 Anchor Books/Random House) See pages 303-324

102 Time Magazine *Mass Suicide at Jonestown: 30 Years Later* (2008) – See the article and photo essay here - http://www.time.com/time/photogallery/0,29307,1859872,00.html | Also check out this interview with one of the survivors from the airstrip: http://www.time.com/time/arts/article/0,8599,1859903-1,00.html

103 Robert Payne *Ancient Rome* (1966 American Heritage Inc/iBooks) See pages 63-82 | Also see: Tom Holland *Rubicon: The Last Years of the Roman Republic* (2003 Anchor Books/Random House) Pages 6-8

104 The full story is in the Book of Exodus, Chapters 19 and 20

105 See Rashi's commentary to Exodus 19:9, "You can't compare hearing the messenger to hearing the King. We want to see our king!"

106 Deuteronomy 4:32-33

107 Bernard Lewis *The Middle East: A Brief History of the Last 2,000 Years* (1995 Touchstone/Simon & Schuster) See Chapters 1-3

The Accuracy of the Torah's Transmission

108 The Hebrew date was the 7th of Adar, 2488. *The Living Torah*, by Aryeh Kaplan, Mozniam Publishing Corporation, 1981

109 Deuteronomy 31:24-26, check out the Talmud in Bava Basra 14a, there are different opinions as to where Moses' Torah was actually kept

110 See Maimonides, Mishna Torah, Laws of Writing a Sefer Torah, Chapter 7, Section 2

111 For the complete list, see Maimonides, Mishna Torah, Laws of Writing a Sefer Torah, Chapter 10, Section 1

112 The Talmud mentions other customs, but this method of reading the entire Torah once a year is the accepted norm.

113 I found this biographical information in an excellent obituary posted here: http://agmk.blogspot.com/2007/02/r-mordechai-breuer-ztll-master-masoret.html

114 The study by Rabbi Breuer is from an excellent article by Rabbi Dovid Lichtman, you can download it here - http://www.pdfgeni.com/book/torah-it-pdf.html and it is reprinted in the appendix

115 The differences are listed in Rabbi Lichtman's article

116 See the obituary cited in note 113

117 Quoted from the *Interpreter's Dictionary of the Bible*, Keith R. Crim and George A. Buttrick, Abingdon Press, October 1976 (I quoted an article, "Accuracy of our Torah Text," written by Aish HaTorah's Discovery Seminar. The article references the quote from the Interpreter's Dictionary of the Bible. You can see the article here: http://www.aish.com/h/sh/tat/48969731.html)

118 http://www.christianitytoday.com/ct/2006/october/23.51.html?start=3

119 Josh McDowell, *Evidence that Demands a Verdict*, page 44, Campus Crusade for Christ, Inc. (1972) – the book has been revised a reprinted. See note 117

Esther, Purim, and the Nazis

120 Definition of Amalek: Rav Tzadok HaCohen (1823 – 1900), *Yisrael Kedoshim* pages 94-95 – I added the outline numbers

121 http://www.pelicanpub.com/proddetail.asp?prod=1589801369 - Quoting Rauschning as a credible source is problematic and some scholars doubt his claims. Many of these quotes are taken from Rauschning's book, *Hitler Speaks*. *Hitler Speaks* is of dubious origin and some consider it a fabrication or Allied war propaganda. Some scholars consider Rauschning legitimate however, and in any event; these quotes are similar to statements quoted by others. (See http://www.ihr.org/jhr/v04/v04p378_Weber.html)

122 Excerpts from H. Rauschning, "The Voice of Destruction."

123 Talmud in Megilah 6B

124 See the GRA, Rabbi Yaakov Emden, and many others. In the Early Middle Ages Germany was spelled with two 'm's – Germamia.

125 *The Rise and Fall of the Third Reich*, W.L. Shirer, page 121

126 http://www.historyorb.com/europe/bismarck2.shtml

127 *Inside the Third Reich*, Albert Speer, Simon & Schuster (April 1, 1997) Published in 1969 and translated into English in 1970.

128 Newsweek, October 28, 1946, Foreign Affairs, Page 46

Acknowledgments

I started teaching the Discovery Seminar in the 1990s. I prepared my classes using old transcripts and stole my best lines from the more experienced teachers. As I improved, I added jokes and original research. I continued listening to other presenters however, and adapted my presentation as I heard new insights, new evidence, or better ways to explain the information. If you are a Discovery teacher, I probably ripped you off. If you see your jokes, lines, innovations, insights, or material in this book please forgive me! In seventeen years I sat through hundreds of Discovery Seminars. I tweaked my presentation (and ultimately this book) every time I heard a good idea. I don't remember who said what, where it was said, or when it was. If you find something in here, tell me and I will do my best to cite you in future editions. For now, please accept my sincerest thanks and appreciation.

I owe a huge debt of gratitude to Rabbi Dovid Lichtman from Aish Jerusalem. He read through most of this book's major sections and took the time to critique, source, clarify, and help rewrite areas that seemed murky or confusing. Thank you also to Rabbi Moshe Zeldman for taking my call at three in the morning (his time!) and answering questions. Thank you to Rabbi Shalom Schwartz for the tremendous amount of support, advice, and good will. And thank you to Rabbi

Eric Coopersmith from Aish International for supporting this project and for the beautiful approbation.

I owe a massive thank you to Larissa Zaretsky. She did the type-setting, layout, and design of this book and her attention to detail and professionalism are greatly appreciated. Thank you to Tzvi Lebetkin for designing the cover and continued encouragement. And thank you to Chananel Weiner and all the others who helped with the fundraising.

Over fifty people contributed to get this book published. I am overwhelmed by your generosity and outpouring of support and could have never done this without you. Wow! What can I say? I am blessed to have so many wonderful people in my life and I wish you nothing but success, fulfillment, and happiness in all that you do. Thank you.

And of course, I owe an incredible thank you to my family, especially my wife and children. Thank you for being wonderful.

Acknowledgments
to the Second Edition

It has only been one year since the first edition of *Discover This* and we are already publishing the second. Wow. The quick sales of this book are a testament to the power of these ideas and the important message of the Discovery Seminar.

Fans of the first edition will notice two things. First you will notice that I fixed up the typos. There were a lot of them. I had so much to do when I put out the first edition that a good final read of the manuscript got lost in the mix. Oops. Typos are a fact of life in publishing, but I did my best to fix as many as I could in this edition. Hopefully they are gone.

Second, you will notice that the codes section is completely rewritten. The original edition was good, but it was lacking important research and missed some of the most important peer-reviewed papers in support of the codes. The history of the early research was inaccurate as well. This section has been updated and I think greatly improved. The basic argument is the same, but the conclusion stands on more solid ground.

A big thank you to Harold Gans and Moshe Zeldman for answering my questions about Torah codes, clarifying specific points, showing me a lot of the new research, and clearing up my fogginess about the original experiments.

A lot of people found typos, but only Larry Lesser sent me a list of almost all of them. He even found a mistake in one of the codes charts! Thank you for sending and for your awesome support of this project.

Thank you again to Esther Zartesky for re-typesetting this edition and to Tzvi Lebetkin for the cover and graphics.

And a special thank you to Rabbi Rafael Sait who was instrumental in getting this edition published.

About the Author

Tzvi Gluckin has been everywhere and done everything. His eclectic tastes and unusual life experiences render him uniquely qualified to discuss a wide array of issues and topics from a fresh and different perspective. His style is unconventional and humorous, his message is powerful and focused, and the experience is inspiring and transformative.

Tzvi is often on tour, speaking to audiences all over the world on a wide range of topics. He is the author of four great books including *Knee Deep in the Funk: Understanding the Connection Between Spirituality and Music* and *Everything You Want Is Really Jewish*. He also recorded *Jewish Roots Music*, a CD of original music. He served in the Israeli Army, holds a B.M.

in Jazz Studies from the New England Conservatory of Music, and received his rabbinical ordination from Rabbi Noah Weinberg *ztz'l* at Aish HaTorah in Jerusalem. He lives in Boston with his wife and children.

Find out more about Tzvi. Bring him to your town. Visit at www.gluckin.com to learn more.

Sponsors of the First Edition

Mr. and Mrs. Robert and Joan Gluckin
AJ Ginsburg
The Simnegar Family
Yitzchak, Marissa, and Yehoshua Finch
Davida and David Zimble and sons

The Sternberg Family
Dr. and Mrs. Ya'aqob Freedman and Family
Anonymous Friends of the Gluckins

Adam Sheps & Rachel Lohr
Joseph, Arielle & Yakira Jaspan
Michal and Ely Lenik
Mr. and Mrs. Marc Rossen and Family
Rivkah Krawiecz
Rabbi Shlomo and Karen Hochberg
Alina and Zave Monisov
Sharon, Rony and Shapiro Family

Honor Roll

Sarah Blisko
S.A.M (Simone, Adam, Michelle)
Danny and Sara Wolfe and Family
Rabbi and Mrs. Judah Mischel and Family
Steven "Koop" Kostick
Daniel Lozovatsky
Binyamin and Marsha Brecher and Family
Alex Rikun

And an extra special thank you to the more than 30 people (in addition to this list) who contributed to make this important project a reality. THANK YOU.

Order more copies of
***Discover This* today!**

Single orders and bulk rate discounts are available.
Inquire today.

**Bring the Discovery Seminar to your
community or campus.
Book Tzvi as your speaker.**

For more information about books and bookings,
visit www.gluckin.com or
email Tzvi directly at tzvi.gluckin@gmail.com.

Made in the USA
Charleston, SC
30 December 2011